HOW TO WRITE BETTER RÉSUMÉS AND COVER LETTERS

by
Pat Criscito, CPRW

President and Founder
ProType, Ltd., Colorado Springs
and author of Barron's
Résumés in Cyberspace,
Designing the Perfect Résumé,
and *Guide to Distance Learning*

BARRON'S

The résumés in this book are real résumés used by real people to get real jobs. The names and contact information have been changed to protect their privacy.

All web site addresses in this book were current on the date of publication. Because of the dynamic nature of the Internet, URLs can change. If you cannot find a site with the published address, use a good search engine to locate an up-to-date address.

All inquiries should be addressed to:
Barron's Educational Series, Inc.
250 Wireless Boulevard
Hauppauge, New York 11788
http://barronseduc.com

Library of Congress Catalog Card No.: 2003044321

International Standard Book No.: 0-7641-2494-3

Library of Congress Cataloging-in-Publication Data

Criscito, Pat, 1953–
    How to write better resumes and cover letters / by Pat Criscito.
        p. cm.
    Includes index.
    ISBN 0-7641-2494-3
        1. Résumés (Employment) 2. Job hunting. I. Title.

 HF5383.C742 2003
 650.14'2--dc21

                                                                2003044321

PRINTED IN THE UNITED STATES OF AMERICA
9 8 7 6 5 4 3 2

Contents

About the Author

Pat Criscito is a Certified Professional Résumé Writer with more than 25 years of experience and résumé clients in 42 countries. As the president and founder of ProType, Ltd., in Colorado Springs, she has written more than 15,000 résumés in her career and speaks nationally on the subject, appearing regularly on television and radio shows, as well as at Harvard, Yale, Tulane, SMU, Thunderbird, and other major universities.

Pat is also the author of Barron's *Designing the Perfect Résumé* (a comprehensive idea book for designing your paper résumé), *Résumés in Cyberspace* (your complete guide to a computerized job search), and *Guide to Distance Learning*. She is a contributing writer to *The Wall Street Journal*'s *careerjournal.com, The Boston Globe, Colorado Springs Business Journal,* and other publications.

Because of her research, Pat is always on the cutting edge of the employment world. She interviews human resource managers across the country and understands what they are looking for in a résumé and how to get a résumé read. In her books, Pat teaches you how to be successful in your job search and how to create and use electronic résumés. In this book, she passes on her expert knowledge of the résumé writing process from an insider's perspective.

Pat is a member of the National Résumé Writers' Association *(www.nrwa.com)* and sits on their board of directors as an officer. For more information and to access the hyperlinks from this book in a handy online format, check her web site at *www.patcriscito.com.* You will also find downloadable versions of all the forms in this book at the same site.

Chapter 1

So, Just What Is the Perfect Résumé?

The *perfect* résumé is the one that fits your personality in both design and wording, tempered of course by the unique expectations of your industry. It must be designed and written in such a way that it stands out in a stack of résumés on a busy executive's desk. It will help you get that all-important interview by making a strong first impression and then by keeping that attention with dynamic sentences that convey your knowledge, skills, and abilities. It's that simple.

Having said that, you should know that writing your résumé is often one of the most difficult things you will ever do! Think about it . . . you must turn your life history into a one- or two-page advertisement that highlights a lifetime of experience, accomplishments, and education. Since we have been taught all of our lives not to brag, most people find this ultimate brag piece difficult to write.

Even if you have already made a first attempt at writing a résumé, it may not meet the expectations of today's discerning hiring manager. The National Résumé Writers' Association *(www.nrwa.com)* publishes a test to help job seekers decide whether their résumés are ready for a job search. With their permission, let's evaluate your old résumé's effectiveness. Put a checkmark by every box that applies to you.

- ❑ My résumé uses the same marketing techniques used by companies to sell my unique "brand" to employers.
- ❑ My résumé is packed with industry-specific language and crucial keywords.
- ❑ My résumé emphasizes and quantifies my achievements to show not only what I have done, but also *how well* I have done it.
- ❑ My résumé uses varied action verbs and powerful marketing phrases.

> *The perfect résumé is the one that fits your personality in both design and wording, tempered by the expectations of your industry.*

1

❑ My résumé contains superior grammar, spelling, sentence structure, and punctuation.

❑ My résumé emphasizes how I will benefit employers and meet their precise needs.

❑ My résumé engages the reader from the outset and maintains interest throughout.

❑ My résumé clearly communicates my job target and the key strengths I bring to the table within the first few lines of text.

❑ My résumé utilizes accomplishment statements in a compelling way.

❑ My résumé communicates and targets my key transferable skills.

❑ My résumé minimizes my potential weaknesses and turns negative "red flags" into positive assets.

❑ My résumé uses an eye-catching, inviting, and original design (not a template).

❑ My résumé includes ASCII (plain-text) and scannable versions to enable e-mail, Internet, and electronic distribution/storage.

❑ My résumé uses the most effective format, style, and strategy for my particular situation.

How did you do? If you checked 13–14 boxes, your résumé writing abilities appear to be sound. You can still benefit from some of the strategies and tips in this book, or you might want to avail yourself of a critique from a professional résumé writer to be sure you didn't miss anything important.

If you checked 10–12 boxes, you have some distinct abilities that will help you write a résumé more solidly than most. Without the help of this book, however, you may leave out some critical components that can cost you interviews. Optimize your results by following all 12 steps in this book.

If you checked less than 10 boxes, you need this book! You will miss opportunities that may be perfect for you unless you apply all the suggestions listed.

Writing the Perfect Résumé

Millions of paper and electronic résumés are distributed every day, and they all serve one purpose—to entice potential employers to open their doors for an interview. Every résumé is simply a marketing tool—your own personal advertisement. Just as the value of money is determined by what is printed on a piece of paper—there is a big difference between $1 and $100 bills—so is the value of your résumé determined by its content and format.

In my own résumé writing practice, I designed a 12-step résumé writing process over the years to help me clarify the experience, accomplishments, skills, education, and other background information of my clients and then to condense that person's life onto paper to create the perfect advertisement, always keeping in mind both the reader and the industry's expectations.

In 1997, I shared that experience with my readers in a shortened form in the first edition of *Résumés in Cyberspace*. My 12-step writing process was then excerpted from the book in *The Wall Street Journal*'s *National Employment Business Weekly* and was selected by their editors for the "Ten Best Articles of the Year" award. It is now permanently archived at *The Wall Street Journal*'s *careerjournal. com* web site.

With this book, I wanted to give you the whole story, to teach you how to create the perfect résumé from beginning to end. In this book you will find insider information from the world of résumé writers. You will learn:

- How to focus your résumé (Chapter 2—Step 1)

- How to define educational experiences to your advantage (Chapter 3—Step 2)

- How to research other sources to help you describe your past experience (Chapter 4—Step 3)

- How to fill your résumé with the buzzwords of your industry and make your résumé pop up in a keyword search in an electronic résumé database (Chapter 5—Step 4)

- How to organize your experience and describe your duties (Chapter 6—Step 5)

- How to emphasize your accomplishments (Chapter 7—Step 6)

- How to refine your information to the most relevant experience (Chapter 8—Step 7)

- How to develop dynamic, attention-getting sentences that will grab and keep your reader's attention (Chapter 9—Step 8)

- How to rearrange the information on your résumé so your reader is forced to see your most important items first (Chapter 10—Step 9)

- How to include related information to strengthen your qualifications (Chapter 11—Step 10)

- How to create a qualifications summary that will knock your reader's socks off (Chapter 12—Step 11)

- How to put it all together, including positioning, design, functional versus chronological résumés, executive résumés, and curriculum vitae (Chapter 13—Step 12)

Electronic Résumés

However, this book won't stop there. In order to manage your career today, you need both a paper résumé and an electronic version that can be left in cyberspace to work for you 24 hours a day.

My companion book from Barron's, *Résumés in Cyberspace,* will help you create the perfect electronic résumé, and show you how to use it on the Internet. However, we will introduce the subject in Chapter 14 so you have a general idea of what makes an electronic version of your résumé different and how to use it effectively.

Cover Letters

What is a good résumé without an equally good cover letter? Every résumé you send out, whether by mail, fax, or e-mail, needs a cover letter. The last chapter will share some of the more common types and give you guidelines for including the right information to entice a hiring manager to continue reading.

Get Ready, Get Set, Write!

You have a wealth of résumé examples in this book from which to choose. Each chapter will provide you with sample wording to guide your creative process. If you find descriptions that work for you, please feel free to use them as a foundation for the words on your own résumé.

That doesn't mean that you should use every sentence verbatim. Accuracy is paramount in a résumé. Never use wording that you cannot explain or justify in an interview.

According to Edward C. Andler, a "résumé detective" hired by companies to check references, cheating on résumés has become distressingly common. Andler's own surveys suggest that as many as one-third of all people exaggerate their accomplishments, while up to 10% seriously misrepresent their backgrounds or work histories. Don't get caught in that trap.

Throughout the book, you will find forms to help you collect information for your résumé. Please feel free to copy them as needed. If you would like to download PDF, MS Word, or WordPerfect versions of the forms, please go to *www.patcriscito.com* and follow the links to my books. When you see the title of this book, there will be hyperlinks to download the files. There are also lists of the web sites provided in the book so you can quickly hyperlink to each site.

Now, let's get down to the business of writing a *perfect* résumé!

Chapter 2

The first step in writing the perfect résumé is to know what kind of job you will be applying for. A résumé without a focus is never as effective as one that relates to a specific job description. If you don't know what you want to be "when you grow up," now is the time to see a career counselor. He or she can help you define where your skills and interests lie through tests and interest inventories.

You can either pay a professional career counselor for these services or approach your college's career services center for help. Some colleges and universities only work with currently enrolled students, while others provide their services to anyone who ever graduated from their institution. Some of these services are free and others are available for a fee.

For help in finding your alma mater's career services center, check the list of web sites at the end of this chapter. To look into the credentials of a career counselor or coach, check the following web sites:

- Career Masters Institute: *www.cmi.com*
- Certified Career Coaches: *www.certifiedcareercoaches.com*
- Career Coach Institute: *www.careercoachinstitute.com*
- Career Counselors Consortium: *www.careercc.org*
- The Coach Connection: *www.findyourcoach.com*
- National Association of Colleges and Employers: *www.naceweb.org*

Before you begin formal career counseling, you should think about the answers to these questions. Write your answers on paper and take them with you to your first counseling session:

- What kind of work makes me the happiest?

- What part of my job do I dislike the most?

> *A résumé without a focus is never as effective as one that relates to a specific job description.*

7

- What am I really good at doing? (list your talents and strengths)

- Why am I good at these things? (natural talent, hard work, etc.)

- Where would I like to see myself in five years?

- What should I do to reach that goal? (training, education, networking, promotions, etc.)

- What would I do if I lost my job tomorrow? (your Plan B)

Career Planning Internet Resources

The Internet is also a great source for do-it-yourself help. Although often not as effective as seeking help from professionally trained counselors, they can sometimes give you at least enough information to help you determine a focus for your résumé. Here are some of the career planning and assessment sites I recommend:

AllHealth.com *http://www.ivillage.com/quiz/0,,437035,00.html*

Career Advisor . . . . *http://www.careeradvisor.com*

Career and Technical Students Organizations . . . . *http://www.acteonline.org/resource_center/index.cfm*

Career Exploration Links . . . . *http://www.uhs.berkeley.edu/Students/Counseling/index.htm*

Career Interests Game, University of Missouri . . . . *http://career.missouri.edu/article.php?sid=146*

Career Manager, U.S. Department of the Interior . . . . *http://www.doi.gov/octc/index.html*

Career Planning Process . . . . *http://www.bgsu.edu/offices/sa/career/students/ol_career_res.html*

CareerBuilder . . . . *http://www.careerbuilder.com*

College Board Online *http://cbweb9p.collegeboard.org/career/bin/career.pl*

Career Quizes . . . . *http://www.fortune.com/fortune/careers*

Excite Career Profiles . . . . *http://www1.excite.com/home/careers/industry_list/0,15624,,00.html*

IQ and Personality Tests . . . . *http://www.davideck.com*

iVillage Career Quiz . . . . *http://www.ivillage.com/quiz/*

Job Profiles.com . . . . *http://www.jobprofiles.org/index.htm*

JobHuntersBible.com . . . . *http://www.jobhuntersbible.com*

Jobs for America's Graduates . . . . *http://www.jag.org*

Keirsey Character and Temperament Sorter . . . . *http://www.keirsey.com*

Mind Tools . . . . *http://www.mindtools.com/*

NAMSS Online Tests and Assessment Tools *http://www.support4learning.org.uk/jobsearch/assess.htm*

NextSteps.org, Youth Employment Center . . . . *http://www.nextsteps.org*

Princeton Review Online . . . . *http://www.review.com/career*

QueenDom . . . . *http://www.queendom.com*

Quint Careers . . . . *http://www.quintcareers.com/test.html*

Self-Directed Search . . . . *http://www.self-directed-search.com/index.html*

TypeFocus on Careers . . . . *http://www.typefocus.com*

U.S. News Self-Evaluation Questionnaire . . . . *http://www.usnews.com/usnews/work/articles/ccciss.htm*

The Objective Statement

Now that you know what you want to do for a living, take a blank piece of paper and write that objective at the top. This can become your objective statement, should you decide to use one, or be used in the first line of the profile section of your résumé to give your reader a general idea of your area of expertise.

Objectives are not required on a résumé, and often the cover letter is the best place to personalize your objective for each job opening. There is nothing wrong with using an objective statement on a résumé, however, provided it doesn't limit your job choices. As an alternative, you can alter individual résumés with personalized objectives that reflect the actual job title for which you are applying. Just make sure that the rest of your information is still relevant to the new objective.

Never write an objective statement that is not precise. The more specific it is, the better it is. You should name the position you want so specifically that, if a janitor came by and knocked over all the stacks of sorted résumés on a hiring manager's desk, he could put yours back in its right stack without even thinking about it. That means saying:

A marketing management position with an aggressive international consumer goods manufacturer.

instead of:

A position which utilizes my education and experience to mutual benefit.

Here are some examples of specific objective statements for various industries:

- **AIRLINE PILOT:** Career as a United Airlines Flight Officer.

- **APPRAISER (entry-level):** Registered appraiser seeking an apprenticeship with a progressive appraisal service that will provide opportunities to further develop appraisal skills and expand real estate knowledge.

- **CHEF:** An executive chef position in a gourmet a la carte restaurant.

- **CUSTOMER SERVICE:** A customer service position in the airline industry, preferably in the Chicago area.

- **ELECTRICAL ENGINEERING:** A position in electrical engineering at the technician/integration level.

- **FACILITY MANAGEMENT:** A responsible physical security, facility/safety program management position.

- **FLIGHT ATTENDANT:** A career as a flight attendant with United Airlines.

- **GENERAL MANAGEMENT:** A management position where an MBA and 12 years of experience, combined with positive interpersonal skills, initiative, and the capacity to motivate others, can be utilized to mutual benefit.

- **HEALTHCARE MANAGEMENT:** To be an integral part of the management of a progressive, growing, and visionary healthcare organization.

- **INTERNATIONAL MANAGEMENT:** A senior management position in a marketing or related capacity for a multinational company with operations in Latin America.

- **MARKETING:** A challenging marketing and/or public relations position that utilizes international experience and allows fulfillment of a desire to grow with a dynamic company whose vision is truly global.

- **MARKETING MANAGEMENT:** A marketing management position with the opportunity to develop and implement marketing strategies that will promote innovative products and/or services. Or: A management position in international sales/marketing in the entertainment industry.

- **MEDICAL ASSISTANT:** A position as a medical assistant that will also utilize back office skills and experience. Or: To work in a medical office where I can utilize my skills as a Registered Medical Assistant and improve my abilities in both back and front office procedures.

- **PARKS AND RECREATION:** A permanent parks and recreation position that will utilize my knowledge, skills, and experience in outdoor education, natural resource interpretation, and/or park maintenance.

- **PHARMACEUTICAL SALES:** Eager to make the transition into pharmaceutical sales where a dynamic personality and strong work ethic could be used to grow market share and increase the profitability of a territory. Or: A challenging and rewarding career in pharmaceutical sales.

- **RESPIRATORY THERAPIST:** Registered Respiratory Therapist desiring a position with a progressive hospital that will provide opportunities to further develop my leadership and teaching skills, expand my knowledge, and further my clinical skills.

- **RETAIL:** A retail kiosk coordinator position with AT&T Wireless Services.

- **SALES:** A sales and marketing position with the opportunity for advancement into management. Or: An account executive position focusing on new business development opportunities.

- **SECRETARIAL:** To build a career in the secretarial field.

- **SEMICONDUCTOR MANUFACTURING:** A position with Intel as a Process Engineering Technician. Or: A position as a clean-room operator or an entry-level maintenance technician position.

- **SOFTWARE DEVELOPMENT:** A responsible position in software requirements analysis, testing, or training. Or: A challenging entry-level, object-oriented software development position.

- **SPORTS MANAGEMENT:** A challenging position in sports management and/or training in a hotel or resort.

- **SYSTEMS ENGINEERING:** A systems engineering position combining outstanding customer and communication skills with leading-edge information technology experience. Particularly interested in emerging system requirements engineering and architecture methodologies, strategic planning for information technology, and business process re-engineering for technology insertion.

- **TRAINING:** A challenging opportunity in corporate or industrial training.

You will notice that occasionally the job title is capitalized as if it were a proper noun. You have some creative license when you write and design a résumé, just like advertising copywriters do. You can choose to capitalize the job title to make it stand out, or you can use the grammatical conventions of capitalizing it only when you personify the title, as I did in the airline pilot and respiratory therapist objectives.

College Career Service Centers

As I mentioned, if you are presently a student at a college or university, your career services center is a great place to start a job search. In addition to skills and interest assessments, many of these schools maintain a résumé database of all their students that can be accessed by companies worldwide.

College career service centers are connected with many employers who list entry-level job openings and internships available to students of that particular school in job banks. Take advantage of those internships and other work experiences long before your graduation. Join student chapters of professional associations, like the American Marketing Association, American Geological Association, and so on. Doing so will produce marketable keywords that will help your electronic résumé pop to the top in a keyword search.

Sometimes colleges offer reciprocal services to students of other schools, but the only way to find out is to make a telephone call to the career center of the school nearest you. Alumni associations are another good place to start. There is an Internet site at *http://www.careerresource.net/carserv/* that is an excellent source for hyperlinks to hundreds of college alumni services. Check there first to see what type of support your alma mater provides. Colleges and universities often offer their alumni the same services as current students, while others limit free services to a year after graduation. Again, check your school just to make sure.

College career service centers may have a home page or a hyperlink from the university's main home page where you can find lists of the career resources available from your particular school. In addition, most major universities and colleges post their own job openings on the school's home page.

As a companion to *Résumés in Cyberspace,* I created a number of hyperlinks to college career service centers. You can access them at my web site (*www.patcriscito.com*) by clicking on *Pat's Books* and following the links.

To locate online information about universities and colleges in general, including the addresses for their home pages, check the following resources:

American Universities . . . . *http://www.clas.ufl.edu/CLAS/american-universities.html*
Career Resource Home Page . . . . *http://www.careerresource.net*
College and University Home Pages *http://www.mit.edu:8001/people/cdemello/univ.html*
CollegeNET . . . . *http://www.collegenet.com*
Peterson's Education Center . . . . *http://www.petersons.com*
U.S. Universities and Community Colleges . . . . *http://www.utexas.edu/world/univ/*

Résumé Sections

In the next chapter, we will begin the process of dividing your information into major headings. Before we start, let's review what those potential titles can be.

For instance, your *objective statement* (should you decide to use one) can be titled:

- Objective
- Goal
- Interests
- Career Objective
- Career Goal
- Job Target

Education is Education, but it could also be:

- Credentials
- Professional Development
- Continuing Education
- Training
- or some other variation

The *profile,* or *qualifications, section* of the résumé can be called:

- Profile
- Qualifications
- Highlights of Qualifications
- Expertise
- Strengths
- Summary
- Synopsis
- Background
- Professional Background
- Executive Summary
- Highlights
- Overview

- Professional Overview
- Capsule
- Keyword Profile

The *experience section* could be headlined:

- Experience
- Relevant Experience
- Professional Experience
- Work History
- Employment History
- Employment Summary
- History
- Professional History
- Related Employment
- Business Experience
- Employment Record
- Career History

When you pull out your *achievements* into a separate section, you can use any of the following subtitles:

- Accomplishments
- Representative Accomplishments
- Related Accomplishments
- Highlights of Accomplishments
- Achievements in the same combinations

You might have noticed the addition of *Related* or *Relevant* before some titles. Use these adjectives when you want to drop some of your experience and focus on a certain industry or job function. Remember, your résumé is just an advertisement. It's not intended to give your reader every ingredient in the soup can. Its purpose is to provide enough information to prompt a hiring manager to pick up the telephone and call you for an interview. You can leave off entire jobs in a résumé. By using the words *related* or *relevant,* you automatically tell your reader that there is more to the story but you have intentionally chosen to leave something out because you thought it would be a waste of the reader's time.

Chapter 3

The second step in writing a résumé is to think about your education. That means all of your training and not just formal education (college, university, or trade school). The education section of your résumé will include degrees, continuing education, professional development, seminars, workshops, and sometimes even self-study.

Turn to the forms at the end of this chapter and list any education or training that you think might relate. If you participated in college activities or received any honors or completed notable projects that relate directly to your target job, then this is the place to list them.

Showing high school education and activities on a résumé is only appropriate when you are under 20 and have no education or training beyond high school. Once you have completed either college courses or specialized technical training, drop your high school information altogether.

If you are a recent college graduate and have little relevant experience, your education section will be placed at the top of your résumé. As you gain more experience, your education almost always gravitates to the bottom.

There is an exception to every rule in the résumé business, however, so use your common sense. If you are trying to change careers and recently went back to school to obtain new credentials, your education section will appear at the top of the résumé even if you have years of experience. Think about your strongest qualifications and make certain they appear in the top half of page one of your résumé.

Which Came First . . .

How you choose to list your school and degree can make a difference in how the reader perceives the importance of each item. For instance, in the following

> There is an exception to every rule in the résumé business!

education section, the name of the university is prestigious, so I chose to list it first so the reader focused on the school. The job seeker had little real experience, so I provided valuable keywords by listing areas of study under each major. The GPA was relevant because he was competing for jobs through the school's career services center, which required GPAs on all résumés.

SOUTHERN METHODIST UNIVERSITY, Cox School of Business, Dallas, Texas
Bachelor of Business Administration, May 1997
- *Major in Management Information Systems* (166 credit hours, GPA 3.9): Database Design and Administration, Business Computer Programming, Advanced Programming Techniques, Systems Analysis Design, Information Systems in Organizations, and Telecommunication Design and Policy.
- *Minor in International Business:* Introduction to World Cultures, International Politics, International Economics, and the Global Perspective.
- *Awards:* SMU Scholarship, Who's Who Among Students in American Universities and Colleges.
- Selected for a special Electronic Commerce Honors Course that provided in-depth, hands-on experience in the use of the Internet to help companies achieve competitive advantage, transform relationships with customers, suppliers, and business partners, and empower global business.
- Completed a year-long mentoring program with a senior executive at Southwestern Bell as part of the SMU Business Associates Program.
- *Honors:* Beta Gamma Sigma National Honor Society for Collegiate Schools of Business, Alpha Iota Delta honorary member of Decision Sciences Institute, Golden Key Honor Society, Financial Management Association National Honor Society, Alpha Chi National Honor Society.

When the degree is more important than the university where it was earned, list your education with the degree first. Prioritize your degrees in order of importance, like this:

Ph.D. IN AEROSPACE ENGINEERING (2002)
University of Maryland, College Park, Maryland
- Dissertation: *The Optimization of Engine-Integrated Hypersonic Waveriders with Steady State Flight and Static Margin Constraints*
- Received a four-year postgraduate research assistantship in the Hypersonic Research Group

MASTER OF BUSINESS ADMINISTRATION, FINANCE (2000)
The Pennsylvania State University, University Park, State College, Pennsylvania
- Graduated *magna cum laude* with a GPA of 3.93
- Graduate Student Association Representative for the MBA program (1998 – 1999)
- Awarded a Graduate Assistantship in the Real Estate Department during the final semester

BACHELOR OF SCIENCE IN NURSING (2000)
Beth-El College of Nursing and Health Sciences, University of Colorado, Colorado Springs, Colorado
- Recipient of the Outstanding BSN Student Award for outstanding leadership, clinical, and academic achievement (May 2000)
- Hand picked by the university's nursing faculty to help teach Aging Simulations (February 1999)
- Beth-El College of Nursing nominee for the UCCS Student Achievement Award (May 2000)

The Devil's in the Details

Details, details, details . . . they really do matter. Something as simple as a date in your education can affect your job search. For instance, writing from-to dates (1999 – 2001) implies that you did not graduate. If you graduated with a degree, list only the year you graduated (2001). Computerized applicant tracking systems (like Resumix) are programmed to show that you have college study but not a degree if they see from-to dates.

If you are searching for a job that will utilize special language skills, cross-cultural experience, or international travel, the fact that you studied abroad or completed a foreign exchange program will be an important addition to your résumé. Study abroad falls under the education category, while travel for recreation's sake could be included in a separate "International Experience" section on your résumé, if you are searching for a job that would make that experience valuable.

STUDIES ABROAD

Loyola University, Rome, Italy (Spring 1999)
• Classroom study integrated with European field experiences

ITESM, Monterrey, Mexico (Summer 1998)
• Intensive Spanish language and Mexican culture studies

When you did not complete a degree but have some college study, you can list the degree with the qualification that you have a certain number of credits left to finish, as in the first sample below, or classify the section as "Undergraduate Studies" like the second sample.

BACHELOR OF SCIENCE, MARKETING (1996 – 1999)
Hawaii Pacific University, Honolulu, Hawaii
• Two credits short of completing an undergraduate degree
• Selected for the Dean's List
OR . . .

UNDERGRADUATE STUDIES

Pikes Peak Community College, Colorado Springs, Colorado
• Banking and Finance Program (2 semesters, full-time)
• Early Childhood Education (3 semesters, full-time)
• Course work included: Communications I and II, Minorities, American Indian, Human Relations

Northern Virginia Community College, Fairfax, Virginia
• Liberal Arts Program (1 semester, full-time)
• Course work included: English Composition, History/Western Civilization II

Colorado Mountain College, Glenwood Springs, Colorado
• Liberal Arts Program (1 semester, full-time)
• Course work included: Introduction to Psychology, Physical Science

I am often asked whether or not to list GPAs on a résumé. My reply is, "If you have a GPA of 3.5 or above, it could help you. From 3.0 to 3.5 neither helps nor hurts you, in most cases. Anything from 2.9 or below can actually hurt your chances of getting an interview." A good rule of thumb to follow is: List your GPA if you are a recent graduate whose résumé will be competing against the résumés of fellow students, provided it's a good GPA. Otherwise, leave it off.

As I've already mentioned, there is an exception to every rule in the résumé business, so use common sense. If nearly every résumé you see for your industry has GPAs listed, then you should list yours, too. For instance, in academic circles, a GPA is often important on a curriculum vita.

Technical and Occupational Training

When you attend a trade school, you receive either a diploma or certificate. This type of schooling can be listed under the "Education" heading or under a separate heading called "Training" or "Technical Training." Following are some examples of various training sections.

MICROSOFT COMPUTER SYSTEM ENGINEER (MCSE) COURSE (2001)
Knowledge Alliance and Executrain, Colorado Springs, Colorado
- Networking Essentials, Administering Windows NT 4.0, Windows NT Core Technologies, Internet-working Microsoft NT using TCP/IP, Enterprise Technologies, Internet Information Systems

HEWLETT-PACKARD TRAINING (1998 – 2000)
- MBTI Business Assessment/Application, Understanding Team Development, Interpersonal Communications, Quality Systems, Conflict Management, Peer Appraisal, Applied One-on-One Task Analysis

ACADEMY GRAPHICS (1997)
- Introduction to CADD Systems for PCB Layout and Program File Editing

LICENSED MASSAGE THERAPIST (2003)
Colorado Institute of Massage Therapy, Colorado Springs, Colorado

EMT CERTIFICATION PROGRAM (1998 to 1999)
Memorial Hospital, Colorado Springs, Colorado
- *General Medicine:* Infants and Children, Chest/Abdomen Injuries, Eye/Face/Neck Injuries, Injuries to the Head and Spine, Musculoskeletal Injuries, Burns, Soft Tissue Injuries, OB/GYN, Allergies, Diabetes, Seizures, Syncope, CPR, Defibrillation, Pharmacology, Patient Assessment/Documentation, Geriatrics, Communication, History and Physical Exam, Medical/Legal/Ethical Issues
- *Emergency Medicine:* Multiple Casualty Incidents, Aeromedical Resources, Extrication and Immobilization, Hazardous Materials, Ambulance Operations, Moving Patients, Trauma Skills, Agricultural and

Industrial Emergencies, Splinting, Bandaging and Dressings, Bleeding, Shock, PASG, Drowning, Near Drowning, Diving Emergencies, Environmental Emergencies, Poisoning, Respiratory Emergencies, Airway/Ventilation/Oxygen, Cardiac Emergencies
- *Psychiatric:* Behavioral Emergencies, Violent Patients, Drugs and Alcohol

Continuing Education

Continuing education, or professional development, shows that you care about lifelong learning and self-development, so think about any relevant training since your formal education was completed.

Relevant is the key word here. Always look at your résumé from the perspective of a potential employer. Don't waste space by listing training that is not directly or indirectly related to your target job.

EMT CONTINUING EDUCATION (1999 to present)
American Medical Response, Colorado Springs, Colorado
- EMT Refresher Course (2001)
- CPR First Responder (2001)
- EKG Recognition and Interpretation (2000)
- Basic Trauma Life Support (2000)
- EMT Basic IV Course (1999)

INGERSOLL-RAND TRAINING PROGRAMS
Quality: Six Sigma, ASQ-CQM Refresher Course (Pareto charts, flow charts, cause and effect tools, checklists, control charts, histograms, scatter diagrams, activity network diagrams, affinity diagrams, interrelationships diagraphs, matrix diagrams, priorities matrices, process decision program charts, and tree diagrams), Management by Fact
Business: Quality of Leadership, Designing High-Performance Organizations, Project Management, Microsoft Project

CHEM NUCLEAR SYSTEMS TRAINING PROGRAMS
Computers: Global Information Systems (ARC INFO)
Business: Communications, Leadership
Environmental: OSHA Hazardous Materials (40 hours), CPR, Radworker II

GENERAL ELECTRIC TRAINING PROGRAMS
Manufacturing: Manufacturing Management Program (MMP), Manufacturing Studies
Quality: NQA-1 Lead Auditor, KT, Root-Cause Analysis, QC Course, TQM, SPC, WorkOut
Engineering: Verification, Design Files, Change Control, Interchangeability

PROFESSIONAL DEVELOPMENT (Education Career)

- Coaching and Team Building Skills for Manager and Supervisor, SkillPath (March 2000)
- Creating Writers through Assessment and Instruction, Six-Trait Writing, Northwest Regional Educational Laboratory, Portland, Oregon (December 1997, April 1999, and February 2000)
- Reproducibles for Beginning Writers, Read-Write Connection (February 2000)
- Getting the Most from Microsoft Office (February 2000)
- Formats and Frameworks, Guided Reading and Writing, National Literacy Coalition (November 1999)
- TOP: Creating Writers, Portland State University, Portland, Oregon (Winter 1998)
- Creating Writers through Assessment and Instruction, Six-Trait Writing (December 1997)
- International Institute of Assessment Leadership, Center for Performance Assessment (35 contact hours, July 1998)
- Teaching to the Standards (Summer 1997)
- Our Future: Expect the Best (Fall 1996)
- Interactive Volleyball Coaching (Summers 1995, 1996)
- Issues Affecting Change, Special Topics Education, Brigham Young University (Summer 1996)
- Volleyball Coaches Clinic, Brigham Young University (August 1996)
- Goals 2000: Performance Assessment (Spring 1996)
- Implementing Standards and Assessments (Fall 1995)
- Curriculum Development and Assessment (Fall 1995)
- Fellow, Colorado Writing Project, Level 1 (Summer 1995)
- Beginning WordPerfect, Northeastern Junior College (Spring 1994)

PROFESSIONAL DEVELOPMENT (Project Management)

- **Management Courses**: Project Management, Sexual Harassment, Security Awareness, Diversity, Team Leader Training, Working I and III, A–Z in Problem Solving, Infoman Change Management, Microsoft Managing Reports and Forms, Electronic Purchase Requisition, Introduction to Telecommunications
- **Technical Courses**: CA-7 Operational Workshop, Enterprise Systems 102 (Midrange), Storage Management Fundamentals (Mainframe/Midrange), TSO/ISPF, CA-7 and CA-11 Job Scheduling Software, Using JCL Effectively, NDM, Lotus 1-2-3, Introduction to LANs, Introduction to OS/2, Lotus Basic Notes Concepts, Microsoft Windows, Microsoft Project, Microsoft Word, Microsoft Access, TCP/IP Introduction
- **Personal Development**: Negotiation/Assertiveness Skills, Seven Habits of Highly Effective People

PROFESSIONAL DEVELOPMENT (Nursing Career)

- Completed yearly accredited continuous education and monthly in-service workshops taught by doctors, drug companies, and equipment manufacturers.
- Received Category I credit for attending the Transcatheter Cardiovascular Therapeutics Symposium (TCT) (1997 and 1999)
- Attended numerous conferences approved by the American Nurses Association
- Completed two years of classroom and clinical experience in non-invasive vascular testing from Cevenar Vascular, Hartford, Connecticut

PROFESSIONAL DEVELOPMENT (Benefits Management Career)

- Completed three parts of the Defined Contribution Course (PA, C1, C2), sponsored by the American Society of Pension Actuaries (ASPA) (1999)
- Attended the annual ASPA conferences and workshops (1988 – present)
- Certified in flexible compensation instruction by the Employers Council on Flexible Compensation (ECFC), requiring five years of experience and a proficiency examination
- Participated in annual ECFC conferences and workshops (1994 – present)
- Completed 40 hours of continuing education per year required by the ASPA and Baird, Kurtz & Dobson (1988 – present)

COLLEGE EDUCATION

Use this form to collect information on your formal college education. Write down everything you can think of, regardless of whether you use it on the final résumé. You will narrow the list later. There is a separate page included in this section for each degree.

DEGREE _____

SCHOOL _____

CITY AND STATE _____

YEARS ATTENDED _____

YEAR GRADUATED _____ GPA _____

MAJOR _____

MINOR _____

THESIS/DISSERTATION _____

_____

~ ~

SIGNIFICANT PROJECTS _____

_____

_____

_____

HONORS, AWARDS, SCHOLARSHIPS, ETC. _____

_____

_____

_____

ACTIVITIES (volunteer, leadership, sports, social groups, etc.) _____

_____

_____

_____

STUDY ABROAD (program, school, country, special areas of study) _____

_____

_____

COLLEGE EDUCATION

Use this form to collect information on your formal college education. Write down everything you can think of, regardless of whether you use it on the final résumé. You will narrow the list later. There is a separate page included in this section for each degree.

DEGREE _____

SCHOOL _____

CITY AND STATE _____

YEARS ATTENDED _____

YEAR GRADUATED _____   GPA _____

MAJOR _____

MINOR _____

THESIS/DISSERTATION _____

_____

~ ~

SIGNIFICANT PROJECTS _____

_____

_____

_____

HONORS, AWARDS, SCHOLARSHIPS, ETC. _____

_____

_____

_____

ACTIVITIES (volunteer, leadership, sports, social groups, etc.) _____

_____

_____

_____

STUDY ABROAD (program, school, country, special areas of study) _____

_____

_____

COLLEGE EDUCATION

Use this form to collect information on your formal college education. Write down everything you can think of, regardless of whether you use it on the final résumé. You will narrow the list later. There is a separate page included in this section for each degree.

DEGREE _____

SCHOOL _____

CITY AND STATE _____

YEARS ATTENDED _____

YEAR GRADUATED _____ GPA _____

MAJOR _____

MINOR _____

THESIS/DISSERTATION _____

_____

~ ~

SIGNIFICANT PROJECTS _____

_____

_____

_____

HONORS, AWARDS, SCHOLARSHIPS, ETC. _____

_____

_____

_____

ACTIVITIES (volunteer, leadership, sports, social groups, etc.) _____

_____

_____

_____

STUDY ABROAD (program, school, country, special areas of study) _____

_____

_____

COLLEGE EDUCATION

Use this form to collect information on your formal college education. Write down everything you can think of, regardless of whether you use it on the final résumé. You will narrow the list later. There is a separate page included in this section for each degree.

DEGREE _____

SCHOOL _____

CITY AND STATE _____

YEARS ATTENDED _____

YEAR GRADUATED _____ GPA _____

MAJOR _____

MINOR _____

THESIS/DISSERTATION _____

_____

~ ~

SIGNIFICANT PROJECTS _____

_____

_____

_____

HONORS, AWARDS, SCHOLARSHIPS, ETC. _____

_____

_____

_____

ACTIVITIES (volunteer, leadership, sports, social groups, etc.) _____

_____

_____

_____

STUDY ABROAD (program, school, country, special areas of study) _____

_____

_____

COLLEGE EDUCATION

Use this form to collect information on your formal college education. Write down everything you can think of, regardless of whether you use it on the final résumé. You will narrow the list later. There is a separate page included in this section for each degree.

DEGREE _____

SCHOOL _____

CITY AND STATE _____

YEARS ATTENDED _____

YEAR GRADUATED _____ GPA _____

MAJOR _____

MINOR _____

THESIS/DISSERTATION _____

_____

~ ~

SIGNIFICANT PROJECTS _____

_____

_____

_____

HONORS, AWARDS, SCHOLARSHIPS, ETC. _____

_____

_____

_____

ACTIVITIES (volunteer, leadership, sports, social groups, etc.) _____

_____

_____

_____

STUDY ABROAD (program, school, country, special areas of study) _____

_____

_____

VOCATIONAL/TECHNICAL TRAINING

Use this form to collect information on your vocational, technical, occupational, and military training. Write down everything you can think of, regardless of whether it relates to your job goal. You will narrow the list later.

NAME OF COURSE _____

PRESENTED BY (company, school, etc.) _____

RESULT (certification, diploma, etc.) _____

DATES ATTENDED _____

~ ~

NAME OF COURSE _____

PRESENTED BY (company, school, etc.) _____

RESULT (certification, diploma, etc.) _____

DATES ATTENDED _____

~ ~

NAME OF COURSE _____

PRESENTED BY (company, school, etc.) _____

RESULT (certification, diploma, etc.) _____

DATES ATTENDED _____

~ ~

NAME OF COURSE _____

PRESENTED BY (company, school, etc.) _____

RESULT (certification, diploma, etc.) _____

DATES ATTENDED _____

~ ~

NAME OF COURSE _____

PRESENTED BY (company, school, etc.) _____

RESULT (certification, diploma, etc.) _____

DATES ATTENDED _____

~ ~

VOCATIONAL/TECHNICAL TRAINING

Use this form to collect information on your vocational, technical, and occupational training. Write down everything you can think of, regardless of whether it relates to your job goal. You will narrow the list later.

NAME OF COURSE _____

PRESENTED BY (company, school, etc.) _____

RESULT (certification, diploma, etc.) _____

DATES ATTENDED _____

~ ~

NAME OF COURSE _____

PRESENTED BY (company, school, etc.) _____

RESULT (certification, diploma, etc.) _____

DATES ATTENDED _____

~ ~

NAME OF COURSE _____

PRESENTED BY (company, school, etc.) _____

RESULT (certification, diploma, etc.) _____

DATES ATTENDED _____

~ ~

NAME OF COURSE _____

PRESENTED BY (company, school, etc.) _____

RESULT (certification, diploma, etc.) _____

DATES ATTENDED _____

~ ~

NAME OF COURSE _____

PRESENTED BY (company, school, etc.) _____

RESULT (certification, diploma, etc.) _____

DATES ATTENDED _____

~ ~

PROFESSIONAL DEVELOPMENT

Use this form to collect information on your professional development and continuing education, including in-services, workshops, seminars, corporate training programs, conferences, conventions, etc. Write down everything you can think of, regardless of whether it relates to your job goal. You will narrow the list later.

NAME OF COURSE _____

PRESENTED BY (company, school, etc.) _____

DATES ATTENDED _____

~~~~~~

NAME OF COURSE _____

PRESENTED BY (company, school, etc.) _____

DATES ATTENDED _____

~~~~~~

NAME OF COURSE _____

PRESENTED BY (company, school, etc.) _____

DATES ATTENDED _____

~~~~~~

NAME OF COURSE _____

PRESENTED BY (company, school, etc.) _____

DATES ATTENDED _____

~~~~~~

NAME OF COURSE _____

PRESENTED BY (company, school, etc.) _____

DATES ATTENDED _____

~~~~~~

NAME OF COURSE _____

PRESENTED BY (company, school, etc.) _____

DATES ATTENDED _____

~~~~~~

NAME OF COURSE _____

PRESENTED BY (company, school, etc.) _____

DATES ATTENDED _____

~~~~~~

PROFESSIONAL DEVELOPMENT

Use this form to collect information on your professional development and continuing education, including in-services, workshops, seminars, corporate training programs, conferences, conventions, etc. Write down everything you can think of, regardless of whether it relates to your job goal. You will narrow the list later.

NAME OF COURSE _____

PRESENTED BY (company, school, etc.) _____

DATES ATTENDED _____

~ ~

NAME OF COURSE _____

PRESENTED BY (company, school, etc.) _____

DATES ATTENDED _____

~ ~

NAME OF COURSE _____

PRESENTED BY (company, school, etc.) _____

DATES ATTENDED _____

~ ~

NAME OF COURSE _____

PRESENTED BY (company, school, etc.) _____

DATES ATTENDED _____

~ ~

NAME OF COURSE _____

PRESENTED BY (company, school, etc.) _____

DATES ATTENDED _____

~ ~

NAME OF COURSE _____

PRESENTED BY (company, school, etc.) _____

DATES ATTENDED _____

~ ~

NAME OF COURSE _____

PRESENTED BY (company, school, etc.) _____

DATES ATTENDED _____

~ ~

Chapter 4

Step 3
Research

What if it has been years since you worked at a job and you can't remember what you did? What if it was just yesterday and you can't remember what you did?! Don't worry. You're not getting old. Most of us forget what we did yesterday, so now we need to come up with some strategies for finding ways to describe your work history.

This chapter will talk about resources for finding job descriptions. The next few chapters will then show you how to use them.

First, get your hands on a written description of the job you wish to obtain and for any jobs you have held in the past, as well as for your current job. If you are presently employed, your human resource department is the first place to look. If not, then go to your local library and ask for a copy of *The Dictionary of Occupational Titles* or the *Occupational Outlook Handbook*. These industry standard reference guides offer volumes of occupational titles and job descriptions for everything from Abalone Divers to Zoo Veterinarians (and thousands in between). You can also find them on the Internet (see next page).

Another resource available at your local library or college career center is *Job Scribe,* a computer software program with more than 3,000 job descriptions. Other places to look for job descriptions include:

- Local government job service agencies
- Professional and technical organizations
- Headhunters (i.e., recruiters)
- Associates who work in the same field
- Newspaper advertisements for similar jobs
- Online job postings (which tend to have longer job descriptions than print ads)

Get your hands on written job descriptions.

31

If you have access to the Internet, you will find some great resources at the following web sites:

- America's Career InfoNet: *www.acinet.org*
- Career Guide to Industries: *www.bls.gov/oco/cg/*
- Careers Online Virtual Careers Show: *www.careersonline.com.au/show/menu.html*
- Dictionary of Occupational Titles: *www.oalj.dol.gov/libdot.htm*
- Exploring Occupations from the University of Manitoba: *www.umanitoba.ca/counselling/careers.html*
- JobProfiles.com: *www.jobprofiles.org*
- Occupational Outlook Handbook: *www.bls.gov/oco/home.htm*
- Occupational Outlook Quarterly: *www.bls.gov/opub/ooq/ooqhome.htm*

Performance evaluations, depending on how well they are written, generally list a description of your major responsibilities, a breakdown of individual tasks, and highlights of your accomplishments. You should *always* keep a folder at home of performance evaluations from every job you have ever held. If you haven't kept them up until now, please start.

Now, make copies of these performance evaluations so you can highlight them as you write your résumé. Use a different colored pen to highlight accomplishments, the things you did above and beyond the call of duty.

Also make copies of the job descriptions you discovered and mark the sentences that describe anything you have done in your past or present jobs. These job descriptions are important sources of keywords, so pay particular attention to nouns and phrases that you can incorporate into your own résumé.

Set these papers aside until Chapter 6 when it will be time to write everything down.

Chapter 5

In today's world of e-mailed and scannable résumés, make sure you know the buzzwords of your industry and incorporate them into the sentences you are about to write. Keywords are the nouns or short phrases that describe any experience and education that might be used to find your résumé in a keyword search of an electronic résumé database. They reflect the essential knowledge, skills, and abilities required to do your job.

They are generally concrete descriptions like:

- C++
- UNIX
- fiber optic cable
- network
- project management
- Spanish
- international

Even well-known company names (AT&T, IBM, Hewlett-Packard) and universities (Harvard, Yale, Princeton, SMU, Stanford, Tulane, Columbia, etc.) are sometimes used as keywords, especially when it is necessary to narrow down an initial search that calls up hundreds of résumés from a résumé database.

Acronyms and abbreviations here can either hurt you or help you, depending on how you use them. One example given to me by an engineer at Resumix was the abbreviation IN. Think about it. IN could stand for *intelligent networks, Indiana,* or the word *in.* It is better to spell out the abbreviation if there could be any possible confusion.

However, if a series of initials is so well known that it would be recognized by nearly everyone in your industry and would not likely be confused with a real word, then the keyword search will

> *Keywords reflect the essential knowledge, skills, and abilities required to do your job.*

probably use those initials (i.e., IBM, CPA, UNIX). When in doubt, always spell it out at least one time on your résumé. A computer only needs to see the combination one time for it to be considered a "hit" in a keyword search.

Soft skills are often not included in search criteria, especially for very technical positions, although I have interviewed some companies that use them extensively for the initial selection of résumés for management positions. For instance, "communicate effectively," "self-motivated," "team player," and so on, are great for describing your abilities and are fine to include in your profile, but concentrate more on your hard skills, especially if you are in a high-tech field.

At the end of this chapter, you will find more examples of keywords for specific industries, although there is no such thing as a comprehensive listing of keywords for any single job. The computerized applicant tracking software used by most companies allows the recruiter or hiring manager to personalize his or her list for each job opening, so it is an evolving process. You will never know whether you have listed absolutely every keyword possible, so focus instead on getting on paper as many related skills as possible, remembering to be absolutely honest and accurate.

The job descriptions and performance evaluations you found in Step 3 are some of the most important sources for keywords. You can also be certain that nearly every noun and some adjectives in a job posting or advertisement will be keywords, so make sure you use those words somewhere in your résumé, using synonyms wherever you can. Just make sure you can justify every word on your résumé—don't exaggerate. If you don't have the experience or skill, don't use the keyword.

The form at the end of this chapter will help you to make a list of the keywords you have determined are important for your particular job search. Also list common synonyms for those words when you can. As you incorporate these words into the sentences of your résumé, check them off.

One caution. Always tell the truth. The minute a hiring manager speaks with you on the telephone or begins an interview, any exaggeration of the truth will become immediately apparent.

It is a bad idea to say, "I don't have experience with MS Word computer software" just to get the words *MS Word* or *computer software* on paper so your résumé will pop up in a keyword search.

In a cover letter, it might be appropriate to say, "I don't have five years of experience in marketing but can add two years of university training in the subject to three years of in-depth experience as a marketing assistant with Hewlett-Packard." That is legitimate reasoning, but anything more manipulative can be hazardous to your job search.

Keywords in Electronic Résumés

Using the right keywords for your particular experience and education is critical to the success of your electronic résumé. Without the right keywords, your résumé will float in cyberspace forever waiting for a hiring manager to find it. If your résumé contains all the right keywords, then you will be among the first candidates whose résumés are reviewed. If you lack only one of the keywords, then your résumé will be next in line after résumés that have them all, and so on.

Remember, your keywords are the specific terminology used in your job that reflect your experience and skills. For instance, *operating room* and *ICU* immediately classify the experience of a nurse, but *pediatric ICU* narrows it down even further.

Don't try to limit your résumé by using fewer words. If your information is longer than one page, a reader looking at a computer screen won't be able to tell, but the computer doing a keyword search will know if a word is not there. Recall, however, that you only need to use a word one time for it to be considered a "hit" in a keyword search. Try to use synonyms wherever possible to broaden your chances of being selected.

You should also understand the difference between a simple keyword search and a concept search. When a recruiter brings up an e-mailed résumé onto the screen and sends the computer on a search for a single word like *marketing*—which one can do in any word processing program with a few clicks of a mouse or function key—he or she is performing a keyword search.

You are also performing a keyword search when you type a word or combination of words into the command line of a search engine like Yahoo! or Google (see example to the left). In that case, sometimes the computer searches entire documents for matches and other times it looks only at headers or extracts from the files.

A concept search, on the other hand, can bridge the gap between words by reading entire phrases and then using sophisticated artificial intelligence to interpret what is being said, translating the phrase into a single word, like *network*, or a combination of words, like *project management*.

For example, in a simple keyword search on "Manager of Product Sales," ordinary software would return a match on a candidate's résumé that reads "worked for a Manager of Product Sales." Using a concept search, Resumix can distinguish between this résumé and another candidate's résumé that indicated "served as a Manager of Product Sales."

The software that extracts data from scanned and e-mailed résumés and Web sources is incredibly sophisticated. Resumix, one of the most widely used recruiting and hiring systems now owned by Yahoo!, reads the grammar of noun, verb, and adjective combinations and extracts the information for placement on the form that will become your entry in a résumé database. Its expert system extraction engine uses a complex knowledge base of more than 197,000 rules and over ten million résumé terms. It recognizes grammatical structure variations, including synonyms and context within natural language text.

It even knows the difference between *Harvard Graphics* (a computer software program) and *Harvard* (the university) by its placement on the page and its relationship to the header that precedes it *(Computer Skills* or *Education)*.

Because of this complicated logic, and because each company and each hiring manager has the ability to personalize the search criteria for each job opening, it is impossible to give you a concrete list of the thousands of possible keywords that could be used to search for any one job.

For instance, StorageTek, a high-tech company in Louisville, Colorado, graciously conducted a keyword search for me of their Resumix database and brought up the following criteria from two different hiring managers for the same job title (see next page). These are keywords extracted from real job requisitions written by hiring managers.

FINANCIAL ANALYST/SENIOR ACCOUNTANT:

REQUIRED:
- BS in finance or accounting with 4 years of experience or
- MBA in related field with 2 years of relevant experience
- certified public accountant
- forecasting

DESIRED:
- accounting
- financial
- trend analysis
- financial statement
- results analysis
- trends
- strategic planning
- develop trends
- financial modeling
- personal computer
- microcomputers
- DCF
- presentation skills
- team player

REQUIRED:
- BS in finance or accounting with 4 years of experience or
- MBA in related field with 2 years of relevant experience
- accounting
- financial reporting
- financial statement
- Excel

DESIRED:
- ability
- customer
- new business
- financial analysis
- financial
- forecasting
- process improvement
- policy development
- business policies
- PowerPoint
- Microsoft Word
- analytical ability

Sample Keywords

You can see why it is so difficult to give definitive lists of keywords and concepts. However, it is possible to give you samples of actual keyword searches used by the recruiters at StorageTek to give you some ideas.

Let me emphasize again that you should list only experience you actually have gained. Do not include the keywords on the following pages in your résumé just because they are listed here.

ACCOUNT EXECUTIVE

REQUIRED:
- BS degree
- 3 years technical selling experience
- Fortune 500 account management experience
- sales
- storage industry
- solution selling

DESIRED:
- Siebel
- quota levels
- VAD
- VAR

ACCOUNTING ANALYST

REQUIRED:
- BA or MBA
- 2–4 years of experience
- asset management
- SAP
- accounting

DESIRED:
- fixed assets
- capital assets
- corporate tax
- US GAAP

BASE SALES REPRESENTATIVE

REQUIRED:
- 2–4 years of sales or contract management experience
- 2+ years of telemarketing or telesales experience

DESIRED:
- Siebel
- storage industry

BUSINESS MANAGER, CENTRAL ARCHIVE MANAGEMENT

REQUIRED:
- BS in engineering or computer science
- 10 years of related engineering and/or manufacturing experience
- strategic planning
- network
- product management
- program management

DESIRED:
- business plan
- line management
- pricing
- team player
- CAM

* marketing
* product strategy
* vendor
* general management
* OEM
* profit and loss

BUSINESS OPERATIONS SPECIALIST:

REQUIRED:
* bachelor's degree
* 4 years of directly related experience
* production schedule
* project planning

DESIRED:
* ability to implement
* CList
* data analysis
* off-shift
* team player
* automation
* ability to plan
* customer interaction
* VM
* CMS
* JCL
* REXX
* MVS
* UNIX
* analytical ability
* customer interface
* network
* skills analysis
* automatic tools

DEVELOPMENT ENGINEER, ADVISORY

REQUIRED:
* BS/BA, Masters desired
* 5–10 years mechanical engineering experience
* 10+ years experience in hardware design
* EMC/EMI debug
* mechanical design
* tape drive

DESIRED:
- DFSS (Design for Six Sigma)
- ANSYS or Metlab
- mechanisms design
- shock
- vibration
- NARTE
- tape library
- data storage

FINANCIAL ANALYST, STAFF

REQUIRED:
- BS in Finance or Accounting
- 1–2 years related experience
- customer-focused experience
- excellent written communication skills
- collection
- financial forecast
- financial modeling
- financial reporting
- financial consolidation
- reconciliation

DESIRED:
- international finance
- hyperion consolidation software
- channel experience

ORDER SPECIALIST

REQUIRED:
- BS degree
- 1–3 years experience
- order administration
- order fulfillment
- invoice processing
- Microsoft Word
- Excel

DESIRED:
- database

PROJECT MANAGER, HUMAN RESOURCES

REQUIRED:
- bachelor's degree in human resources, business, or related field
- 6 years broad experience

DESIRED:
- communications
- project management
- milestone development
- time management
- credibility
- recruiting
- long-range planning
- sourcing

SECRETARY III

REQUIRED:
- high school education or equivalent
- 5 years of experience
- typing skill of 55–60 wpm
- interpersonal skills
- oral communication

DESIRED:
- administrative assistance
- clerical
- data analysis
- file maintenance
- material repair
- PowerPoint
- project planning
- reports
- screen calls
- troubleshoot
- answer phones
- communication skills
- document distribution
- mail sorting
- Microsoft Word
- presentation
- publication
- schedule calendar
- secretarial

- appointments
- confidential
- edit
- material
- policies and procedures
- problem solving
- records management
- schedule conference
- telephone interview

SOFTWARE ENGINEER—EMBEDDED, ADVISORY LEVEL

REQUIRED:
- BS or MS degree in one of the computer sciences or engineering
- 12–14 years of experience minimum
- controller architecture design experience
- disk controller
- fiber channel
- SCSI design
- embedded systems

DESIRED:
- open systems
- product development

SOFTWARE ENGINEER—EMBEDDED, STAFF

REQUIRED:
- BS or MS degree in one of the computer sciences or engineering
- 3–5 years of experience minimum
- C
- embedded systems
- realtime

DESIRED:
- pSOS
- iCLinux

SOFTWARE ENGINEER, SENIOR

REQUIRED:
- BS/MS in engineering, computer science or closely related field
- 8 to 9 years of experience

DESIRED:
- C
- customer
- hiring/firing
- prototype
- structured design
- code development
- DASD
- methodology
- real time
- supervision
- communication skills
- experiment design
- problem solving
- software design
- testing

SYSTEMS ENGINEER, SENIOR

REQUIRED:
- BS degree in related field
- 8–10 years of experience
- pre-sales
- systems engineering
- MVS
- data storage

DESIRED:
- systems configuration
- capacity planning
- DFHSM
- HSC
- presentation skills

KEYWORDS

❏ Keyword:_____
   ❏ Synonym:_____
   ❏ Synonym:_____

❏ Keyword:_____
   ❏ Synonym:_____
   ❏ Synonym:_____

❏ Keyword:_____
   ❏ Synonym:_____
   ❏ Synonym:_____

❏ Keyword:_____
   ❏ Synonym:_____
   ❏ Synonym:_____

❏ Keyword:_____
   ❏ Synonym:_____
   ❏ Synonym:_____

❏ Keyword:_____
   ❏ Synonym:_____
   ❏ Synonym:_____

❏ Keyword:_____
   ❏ Synonym:_____
   ❏ Synonym:_____

❏ Keyword:_____
   ❏ Synonym:_____
   ❏ Synonym:_____

❏ Keyword:_____
   ❏ Synonym:_____
   ❏ Synonym:_____

❏ Keyword:_____
   ❏ Synonym:_____
   ❏ Synonym:_____

❏ Keyword:_____
   ❏ Synonym:_____
   ❏ Synonym:_____

❏ Keyword:_____
   ❏ Synonym:_____
   ❏ Synonym:_____

❏ Keyword:_____
   ❏ Synonym:_____
   ❏ Synonym:_____

❏ Keyword:_____
   ❏ Synonym:_____
   ❏ Synonym:_____

❏ Keyword:_____
   ❏ Synonym:_____
   ❏ Synonym:_____

❏ Keyword:_____
   ❏ Synonym:_____
   ❏ Synonym:_____

❏ Keyword:_____
   ❏ Synonym:_____
   ❏ Synonym:_____

❏ Keyword:_____
   ❏ Synonym:_____
   ❏ Synonym:_____

❏ Keyword:_____
   ❏ Synonym:_____
   ❏ Synonym:_____

❏ Keyword:_____
   ❏ Synonym:_____
   ❏ Synonym:_____

❏ Keyword:_____
   ❏ Synonym:_____
   ❏ Synonym:_____

❏ Keyword:_____
   ❏ Synonym:_____
   ❏ Synonym:_____

❏ Keyword:_____
   ❏ Synonym:_____
   ❏ Synonym:_____

❏ Keyword:_____
   ❏ Synonym:_____
   ❏ Synonym:_____

KEYWORDS

☐ Keyword:_____
   ☐ Synonym:_____
   ☐ Synonym:_____

☐ Keyword:_____
   ☐ Synonym:_____
   ☐ Synonym:_____

☐ Keyword:_____
   ☐ Synonym:_____
   ☐ Synonym:_____

☐ Keyword:_____
   ☐ Synonym:_____
   ☐ Synonym:_____

☐ Keyword:_____
   ☐ Synonym:_____
   ☐ Synonym:_____

☐ Keyword:_____
   ☐ Synonym:_____
   ☐ Synonym:_____

☐ Keyword:_____
   ☐ Synonym:_____
   ☐ Synonym:_____

☐ Keyword:_____
   ☐ Synonym:_____
   ☐ Synonym:_____

☐ Keyword:_____
   ☐ Synonym:_____
   ☐ Synonym:_____

☐ Keyword:_____
   ☐ Synonym:_____
   ☐ Synonym:_____

☐ Keyword:_____
   ☐ Synonym:_____
   ☐ Synonym:_____

☐ Keyword:_____
   ☐ Synonym:_____
   ☐ Synonym:_____

☐ Keyword:_____
   ☐ Synonym:_____
   ☐ Synonym:_____

☐ Keyword:_____
   ☐ Synonym:_____
   ☐ Synonym:_____

☐ Keyword:_____
   ☐ Synonym:_____
   ☐ Synonym:_____

☐ Keyword:_____
   ☐ Synonym:_____
   ☐ Synonym:_____

☐ Keyword:_____
   ☐ Synonym:_____
   ☐ Synonym:_____

☐ Keyword:_____
   ☐ Synonym:_____
   ☐ Synonym:_____

☐ Keyword:_____
   ☐ Synonym:_____
   ☐ Synonym:_____

☐ Keyword:_____
   ☐ Synonym:_____
   ☐ Synonym:_____

☐ Keyword:_____
   ☐ Synonym:_____
   ☐ Synonym:_____

☐ Keyword:_____
   ☐ Synonym:_____
   ☐ Synonym:_____

☐ Keyword:_____
   ☐ Synonym:_____
   ☐ Synonym:_____

☐ Keyword:_____
   ☐ Synonym:_____
   ☐ Synonym:_____

KEYWORDS

❏ Keyword:_____
    ❏ Synonym:_____
    ❏ Synonym:_____

❏ Keyword:_____
    ❏ Synonym:_____
    ❏ Synonym:_____

❏ Keyword:_____
    ❏ Synonym:_____
    ❏ Synonym:_____

❏ Keyword:_____
    ❏ Synonym:_____
    ❏ Synonym:_____

❏ Keyword:_____
    ❏ Synonym:_____
    ❏ Synonym:_____

❏ Keyword:_____
    ❏ Synonym:_____
    ❏ Synonym:_____

❏ Keyword:_____
    ❏ Synonym:_____
    ❏ Synonym:_____

❏ Keyword:_____
    ❏ Synonym:_____
    ❏ Synonym:_____

❏ Keyword:_____
    ❏ Synonym:_____
    ❏ Synonym:_____

❏ Keyword:_____
    ❏ Synonym:_____
    ❏ Synonym:_____

❏ Keyword:_____
    ❏ Synonym:_____
    ❏ Synonym:_____

❏ Keyword:_____
    ❏ Synonym:_____
    ❏ Synonym:_____

❏ Keyword:_____
    ❏ Synonym:_____
    ❏ Synonym:_____

❏ Keyword:_____
    ❏ Synonym:_____
    ❏ Synonym:_____

❏ Keyword:_____
    ❏ Synonym:_____
    ❏ Synonym:_____

❏ Keyword:_____
    ❏ Synonym:_____
    ❏ Synonym:_____

❏ Keyword:_____
    ❏ Synonym:_____
    ❏ Synonym:_____

❏ Keyword:_____
    ❏ Synonym:_____
    ❏ Synonym:_____

❏ Keyword:_____
    ❏ Synonym:_____
    ❏ Synonym:_____

❏ Keyword:_____
    ❏ Synonym:_____
    ❏ Synonym:_____

❏ Keyword:_____
    ❏ Synonym:_____
    ❏ Synonym:_____

❏ Keyword:_____
    ❏ Synonym:_____
    ❏ Synonym:_____

❏ Keyword:_____
    ❏ Synonym:_____
    ❏ Synonym:_____

❏ Keyword:_____
    ❏ Synonym:_____
    ❏ Synonym:_____

KEYWORDS

❏ Keyword:_____
   ❏ Synonym:_____
   ❏ Synonym:_____

❏ Keyword:_____
   ❏ Synonym:_____
   ❏ Synonym:_____

❏ Keyword:_____
   ❏ Synonym:_____
   ❏ Synonym:_____

❏ Keyword:_____
   ❏ Synonym:_____
   ❏ Synonym:_____

❏ Keyword:_____
   ❏ Synonym:_____
   ❏ Synonym:_____

❏ Keyword:_____
   ❏ Synonym:_____
   ❏ Synonym:_____

❏ Keyword:_____
   ❏ Synonym:_____
   ❏ Synonym:_____

❏ Keyword:_____
   ❏ Synonym:_____
   ❏ Synonym:_____

❏ Keyword:_____
   ❏ Synonym:_____
   ❏ Synonym:_____

❏ Keyword:_____
   ❏ Synonym:_____
   ❏ Synonym:_____

❏ Keyword:_____
   ❏ Synonym:_____
   ❏ Synonym:_____

❏ Keyword:_____
   ❏ Synonym:_____
   ❏ Synonym:_____

❏ Keyword:_____
   ❏ Synonym:_____
   ❏ Synonym:_____

❏ Keyword:_____
   ❏ Synonym:_____
   ❏ Synonym:_____

❏ Keyword:_____
   ❏ Synonym:_____
   ❏ Synonym:_____

❏ Keyword:_____
   ❏ Synonym:_____
   ❏ Synonym:_____

❏ Keyword:_____
   ❏ Synonym:_____
   ❏ Synonym:_____

❏ Keyword:_____
   ❏ Synonym:_____
   ❏ Synonym:_____

❏ Keyword:_____
   ❏ Synonym:_____
   ❏ Synonym:_____

❏ Keyword:_____
   ❏ Synonym:_____
   ❏ Synonym:_____

❏ Keyword:_____
   ❏ Synonym:_____
   ❏ Synonym:_____

❏ Keyword:_____
   ❏ Synonym:_____
   ❏ Synonym:_____

❏ Keyword:_____
   ❏ Synonym:_____
   ❏ Synonym:_____

❏ Keyword:_____
   ❏ Synonym:_____
   ❏ Synonym:_____

KEYWORDS

❑ Keyword:_____
   ❑ Synonym:_____
   ❑ Synonym:_____

❑ Keyword:_____
   ❑ Synonym:_____
   ❑ Synonym:_____

❑ Keyword:_____
   ❑ Synonym:_____
   ❑ Synonym:_____

❑ Keyword:_____
   ❑ Synonym:_____
   ❑ Synonym:_____

❑ Keyword:_____
   ❑ Synonym:_____
   ❑ Synonym:_____

❑ Keyword:_____
   ❑ Synonym:_____
   ❑ Synonym:_____

❑ Keyword:_____
   ❑ Synonym:_____
   ❑ Synonym:_____

❑ Keyword:_____
   ❑ Synonym:_____
   ❑ Synonym:_____

❑ Keyword:_____
   ❑ Synonym:_____
   ❑ Synonym:_____

❑ Keyword:_____
   ❑ Synonym:_____
   ❑ Synonym:_____

❑ Keyword:_____
   ❑ Synonym:_____
   ❑ Synonym:_____

❑ Keyword:_____
   ❑ Synonym:_____
   ❑ Synonym:_____

❑ Keyword:_____
   ❑ Synonym:_____
   ❑ Synonym:_____

❑ Keyword:_____
   ❑ Synonym:_____
   ❑ Synonym:_____

❑ Keyword:_____
   ❑ Synonym:_____
   ❑ Synonym:_____

❑ Keyword:_____
   ❑ Synonym:_____
   ❑ Synonym:_____

❑ Keyword:_____
   ❑ Synonym:_____
   ❑ Synonym:_____

❑ Keyword:_____
   ❑ Synonym:_____
   ❑ Synonym:_____

❑ Keyword:_____
   ❑ Synonym:_____
   ❑ Synonym:_____

❑ Keyword:_____
   ❑ Synonym:_____
   ❑ Synonym:_____

❑ Keyword:_____
   ❑ Synonym:_____
   ❑ Synonym:_____

❑ Keyword:_____
   ❑ Synonym:_____
   ❑ Synonym:_____

❑ Keyword:_____
   ❑ Synonym:_____
   ❑ Synonym:_____

❑ Keyword:_____
   ❑ Synonym:_____
   ❑ Synonym:_____

Chapter 6

Now that you have the basic information gathered for your résumé, you need to create a list of your jobs and write basic sentences to describe your duties. Start by using a separate page at the end of this chapter for each of the jobs you have held for the past 10 or 15 years. You can generally stop there unless there is something in your previous work history that is particularly relevant to the new job you are seeking.

Starting with your present position, list the title of every job you have held, along with the name of the company, the city and state, and the years you worked there. You don't need to list full addresses and zip codes, although you will need to know that information when it comes time to fill out an application. You should use a separate page for each job title even if you worked for the same company in more than one capacity.

By the way, you *can* use a computer. I've had people assume that they had to write this all out in longhand simply because I suggest a separate piece of paper for each job. You can download MS Word, WordPerfect, and PDF files of all the forms in this book by going to my web site at *www.patcriscito.com*.

You can list years only (1996 – present) or months and years (May 1996 – present), depending on your personality. People who are detail oriented are usually more comfortable with a full accounting of their time. Listing years alone covers some gaps if you have worked in a position for less than a full year while the time period spans more than one calendar year. For instance, if you worked from December 1996 through May 1997, saying 1996 – 1997 certainly looks better. If you are concerned about gaps in your work history, then listing years only is to your advantage.

From the perspective of recruiters and hiring managers, most don't care whether you list the months and years or list the years only. However, regardless of which method you choose, be consistent throughout your résumé,

Consistency of style is important on a résumé.

especially within sections. For instance, don't use months some of the time and years alone within the same section. Consistency of style is important on a résumé, since it is that consistency that makes your résumé neat, clean, and easy to read.

Under each job on its separate page, make a list of your duties, incorporating phrases from the job descriptions wherever they apply. You don't have to worry about making great sentences yet or narrowing down your list. Just get the information down on paper.

This is the most time-consuming part of the résumé writing process. Depending on how quickly you write/type, it could take an entire day just for this step. Anything worth doing, however, is worth doing right, so you will want to take the time to do this step right.

Unpaid Experience

Don't forget internships, practicums, and unpaid volunteer work in your experience section. Experience is experience whether you are paid for it or not. If the position or the knowledge you gained is relevant to your current job search, then list it on your résumé.

You can either include unpaid experience along with your paid experience, or you can create a separate section just for your volunteer history, like this:

VOLUNTEER HISTORY

Junior League of Colorado Springs, Colorado Springs, Colorado (1999 – 2003)
Developed goals and action plans, promoted projects to the community, and recruited members. Provided information and training to other league members and educated members on placement opportunities and policies. Attended court hearings and made recommendations to social caseworkers to improve the quality of legal representation for abused children. Raised $30,000 in funds for community projects, reconciled financial statements, and arranged publicity.
- Court Appointed Special Advocate (CASA) Program (August 1999 – May 2003)
- Placement Advisor, Committee Member (June 1998 – May 2000)
- Historian Committee, Chairperson (June 1999 – February 2000)
- Membership Development Committee (August 1998 – May 1999)
- Community Service Corps Committee (January 1997 – May 1998)

Cheyenne Mountain Newcomers Club, Colorado Springs, Colorado (1995 – 1999)
Planned, organized, and coordinated activities for more than 300 members. Maintained membership records and coordinated printing and mailing of directories. Presided at all general and executive board meetings in president's absence.
- First Vice President (December 1998 – May 1999)
- Second Vice President (July 1997 – May 1998)
- General Meetings Chairperson (August 1996 – May 1997)

EXPERIENCE—JOB NO. 1

JOB TITLE _____

NAME OF EMPLOYER _____

CITY AND STATE _____

DATE STARTED _____ DATE ENDED _____

SUMMARY SENTENCE (The overall scope of your responsibility, overview of your essential role in the company, kind of products or services for which you were responsible) _____

_____

_____

_____

_____

NUMBER OF PEOPLE SUPERVISED AND THEIR TITLES OR FUNCTIONS _____

_____

_____

_____

DESCRIPTION OF RESPONSIBILITIES (Don't forget budget, hiring, training, operations, strategic planning, new business development, production, customer service, sales, marketing, advertising, etc.) _____

_____

_____

_____

_____

_____

_____

_____

_____

_____

_____

_____

_____

_____

_____

_____

ACCOMPLISHMENTS (Leave this section blank until Step 6 in Chapter 7) _____

_____

_____

_____

_____

_____

_____

_____

_____

_____

_____

_____

_____

EXPERIENCE—JOB NO. 2

JOB TITLE _____

NAME OF EMPLOYER _____

CITY AND STATE _____

DATE STARTED _____ DATE ENDED _____

SUMMARY SENTENCE (The overall scope of your responsibility, overview of your essential role in the company, kind of products or services for which you were responsible) _____
_____
_____
_____
_____

NUMBER OF PEOPLE SUPERVISED AND THEIR TITLES OR FUNCTIONS _____
_____
_____
_____
_____

DESCRIPTION OF RESPONSIBILITIES (Don't forget budget, hiring, training, operations, strategic planning, new business development, production, customer service, sales, marketing, advertising, etc.) _____
_____
_____
_____
_____
_____
_____
_____
_____
_____
_____
_____
_____
_____
_____
_____
_____

ACCOMPLISHMENTS (Leave this section blank until Step 6 in Chapter 7) _____
_____
_____
_____
_____
_____
_____
_____
_____
_____
_____
_____
_____

EXPERIENCE—JOB NO. 3

JOB TITLE _____

NAME OF EMPLOYER _____

CITY AND STATE _____

DATE STARTED _____ DATE ENDED _____

SUMMARY SENTENCE (The overall scope of your responsibility, overview of your essential role in the company, kind of products or services for which you were responsible) _____
_____
_____
_____
_____

NUMBER OF PEOPLE SUPERVISED AND THEIR TITLES OR FUNCTIONS _____
_____
_____
_____
_____

DESCRIPTION OF RESPONSIBILITIES (Don't forget budget, hiring, training, operations, strategic planning, new business development, production, customer service, sales, marketing, advertising, etc.) _____
_____
_____
_____
_____
_____
_____
_____
_____
_____
_____
_____
_____
_____
_____
_____

ACCOMPLISHMENTS (Leave this section blank until Step 6 in Chapter 7) _____
_____
_____
_____
_____
_____
_____
_____
_____
_____
_____
_____
_____
_____

EXPERIENCE—JOB NO. 4

JOB TITLE _____

NAME OF EMPLOYER _____

CITY AND STATE _____

DATE STARTED _____ DATE ENDED _____

SUMMARY SENTENCE (The overall scope of your responsibility, overview of your essential role in the company, kind of products or services for which you were responsible) _____

_____

_____

_____

_____

NUMBER OF PEOPLE SUPERVISED AND THEIR TITLES OR FUNCTIONS _____

_____

_____

_____

_____

DESCRIPTION OF RESPONSIBILITIES (Don't forget budget, hiring, training, operations, strategic planning, new business development, production, customer service, sales, marketing, advertising, etc.) _____

_____

_____

_____

_____

_____

_____

_____

_____

_____

_____

_____

_____

_____

_____

_____

_____

ACCOMPLISHMENTS (Leave this section blank until Step 6 in Chapter 7) _____

_____

_____

_____

_____

_____

_____

_____

_____

_____

_____

_____

_____

_____

EXPERIENCE—JOB NO. 5

JOB TITLE _____

NAME OF EMPLOYER _____

CITY AND STATE _____

DATE STARTED _____ DATE ENDED _____

SUMMARY SENTENCE (The overall scope of your responsibility, overview of your essential role in the company, kind of products or services for which you were responsible) _____

_____

_____

_____

_____

NUMBER OF PEOPLE SUPERVISED AND THEIR TITLES OR FUNCTIONS _____

_____

_____

_____

_____

DESCRIPTION OF RESPONSIBILITIES (Don't forget budget, hiring, training, operations, strategic planning, new business development, production, customer service, sales, marketing, advertising, etc.) _____

_____

_____

_____

_____

_____

_____

_____

_____

_____

_____

_____

_____

_____

ACCOMPLISHMENTS (Leave this section blank until Step 6 in Chapter 7) _____

_____

_____

_____

_____

_____

_____

_____

_____

_____

_____

_____

EXPERIENCE—JOB NO. 6

JOB TITLE _____

NAME OF EMPLOYER _____

CITY AND STATE _____

DATE STARTED _____ DATE ENDED _____

SUMMARY SENTENCE (The overall scope of your responsibility, overview of your essential role in the company, kind of products or services for which you were responsible) _____
_____
_____
_____
_____

NUMBER OF PEOPLE SUPERVISED AND THEIR TITLES OR FUNCTIONS _____
_____
_____
_____
_____

DESCRIPTION OF RESPONSIBILITIES (Don't forget budget, hiring, training, operations, strategic planning, new business development, production, customer service, sales, marketing, advertising, etc.) _____
_____
_____
_____
_____
_____
_____
_____
_____
_____
_____
_____
_____
_____
_____
_____

ACCOMPLISHMENTS (Leave this section blank until Step 6 in Chapter 7) _____
_____
_____
_____
_____
_____
_____
_____
_____
_____
_____
_____

EXPERIENCE—JOB NO. 7

JOB TITLE _____

NAME OF EMPLOYER _____

CITY AND STATE _____

DATE STARTED _____ DATE ENDED _____

SUMMARY SENTENCE (The overall scope of your responsibility, overview of your essential role in the company, kind of products or services for which you were responsible) _____

_____

_____

_____

_____

NUMBER OF PEOPLE SUPERVISED AND THEIR TITLES OR FUNCTIONS _____

_____

_____

_____

_____

DESCRIPTION OF RESPONSIBILITIES (Don't forget budget, hiring, training, operations, strategic planning, new business development, production, customer service, sales, marketing, advertising, etc.) _____

_____

_____

_____

_____

_____

_____

_____

_____

_____

_____

_____

_____

_____

_____

ACCOMPLISHMENTS (Leave this section blank until Step 6 in Chapter 7) _____

_____

_____

_____

_____

_____

_____

_____

_____

_____

_____

_____

EXPERIENCE—JOB NO. 8

JOB TITLE _____

NAME OF EMPLOYER _____

CITY AND STATE _____

DATE STARTED _____ DATE ENDED _____

SUMMARY SENTENCE (The overall scope of your responsibility, overview of your essential role in the company, kind of products or services for which you were responsible) _____

_____

_____

_____

_____

NUMBER OF PEOPLE SUPERVISED AND THEIR TITLES OR FUNCTIONS _____

_____

_____

_____

_____

DESCRIPTION OF RESPONSIBILITIES (Don't forget budget, hiring, training, operations, strategic planning, new business development, production, customer service, sales, marketing, advertising, etc.) _____

_____

_____

_____

_____

_____

_____

_____

_____

_____

_____

_____

_____

_____

_____

ACCOMPLISHMENTS (Leave this section blank until Step 6 in Chapter 7) _____

_____

_____

_____

_____

_____

_____

_____

_____

_____

_____

_____

_____

EXPERIENCE—JOB NO. 9

JOB TITLE _____

NAME OF EMPLOYER _____

CITY AND STATE _____

DATE STARTED _____ DATE ENDED _____

SUMMARY SENTENCE (The overall scope of your responsibility, overview of your essential role in the company, kind of products or services for which you were responsible) _____

_____

_____

_____

_____

NUMBER OF PEOPLE SUPERVISED AND THEIR TITLES OR FUNCTIONS _____

_____

_____

_____

_____

DESCRIPTION OF RESPONSIBILITIES (Don't forget budget, hiring, training, operations, strategic planning, new business development, production, customer service, sales, marketing, advertising, etc.) _____

_____

_____

_____

_____

_____

_____

_____

_____

_____

_____

_____

_____

_____

_____

ACCOMPLISHMENTS (Leave this section blank until Step 6 in Chapter 7) _____

_____

_____

_____

_____

_____

_____

_____

_____

_____

_____

_____

_____

_____

EXPERIENCE—JOB NO. 10

JOB TITLE _____

NAME OF EMPLOYER _____

CITY AND STATE _____

DATE STARTED _____ DATE ENDED _____

SUMMARY SENTENCE (The overall scope of your responsibility, overview of your essential role in the company, kind of products or services for which you were responsible) _____

_____

_____

_____

_____

NUMBER OF PEOPLE SUPERVISED AND THEIR TITLES OR FUNCTIONS _____

_____

_____

_____

_____

DESCRIPTION OF RESPONSIBILITIES (Don't forget budget, hiring, training, operations, strategic planning, new business development, production, customer service, sales, marketing, advertising, etc.) _____

_____

_____

_____

_____

_____

_____

_____

_____

_____

_____

_____

_____

_____

_____

_____

ACCOMPLISHMENTS (Leave this section blank until Step 6 in Chapter 7) _____

_____

_____

_____

_____

_____

_____

_____

_____

_____

_____

_____

_____

Chapter 7

When you are finished with your work history, go back to each job and think about what you might have done above and beyond the call of duty. What did you contribute to each of your jobs? How did you measure your success? Did you:

- Exceed sales quotas by 150% each month?

- Save the company $100,000 by developing a new procedure?

- Generate new product publicity in trade press?

- Control expenses or cut overhead?

- Expand business or attract/retain customers?

- Improve the company's image or build new relationships?

- Improve the quality of a product?

- Solve a problem?

- Do something that made the company more competitive?

- Make money?

- Save money or time?

- Improve quality or service?

- Increase productivity?

- Improve workplace safety?

- Increase efficiency or make work easier?

Go back to the experience forms at the end of Chapter 6 and write down any accomplishments that show potential employers what you have done in the past, which translates into what you might be able to do for them in the future.

Overused words lose their effectiveness, like a song played on the radio again and again.

61

Quantify whenever possible. Numbers are always impressive. But don't duplicate wording throughout the résumé. If you use dollars in one case, use percentages in another. Overused words lose their effectiveness, like a song played on the radio again and again.

Remember, you are trying to motivate the potential employer to buy . . . you! Convince your reader that you will be able to generate a significant return on their investment in you.

Sample Accomplishment Sentences

Following are some real accomplishments used by real people on real résumés. They are extracted from many different résumés, so don't be surprised if the bullets jump around within the sections. Each bullet is a separate accomplishment. They aren't used in a résumé like they are listed here.

Your achievements won't be identical, but you can use these sentences as a foundation for your own words. Many of the phrases can cross over various industries, but some are specific to a particular job or company.

AVIATION
- Successfully set the standard for safe operations throughout the organization.
- Commended by upper management for mentoring and training junior pilots to improve their technical, tactical, and leadership skills.
- Designated to bring safety operations up to standard only two months before major inspections.
- Twice chosen to perform mid-level management responsibilities while only a junior officer.
- Hand picked to fly local general officers and visiting dignitaries.
- Developed and implemented improvement programs to correct flightline operating deficiencies.

ACCOUNTING
- Developed and implemented numerous improvements to financial reporting, budgeting, and internal controls that supported sales growth of 200%.
- Reduced charge-offs from .2% to .1% and receivables turnover from 50 to 42 days during this period.
- Over a five-year period, lowered overall borrowing costs by 1%.
- Identified $3.5 million in misused funds for return to the USOC.
- Personally recovered $1.423 million in 1997 out of a department total of $1.642 million.
- Audited $10 million in Olympic Games tickets, identifying opportunities to strengthen internal controls, improve operational efficiencies, and save hundreds of thousands of dollars.
- Conducted an analytical review of a $5 million inventory and spearheaded actions to revalue the inventory with material adjustments.
- Succeeded in delivering 25 complete systems to users, including the automation of a formerly paper-based order entry system that increased billing efficiency by 25%.
- Selected to serve on a statewide task force to develop a comprehensive internal controls program.

BAKERY MANAGEMENT
- Evaluated and changed the production schedule of the bakery department to introduce new products, which increased profits and better met customer needs.

BANKING
- Implemented the training rollout for the automated profiling system, a computer-based contact management system that allows bankers to add value to their customer relationships and sell additional business lines.
- Created an inspection process to drive usage of the profiling system by bankers, achieving 45% system use for all customers purchasing product in the first year of implementation.
- Recommended, implemented, and managed an alternative delivery strategy known as dedicated bankers, which increased the percentage of mortgage customers buying additional products from 20% to 40% in only one year.
- Successfully managed a targeted census tract location with high burden ratios and processing costs (ranked second in transaction volume compared to size).
- Increased assets from $60 million to $99.5 million in five years; led the city in annuity sales.
- Determined that small business customers were being underserved and developed a strategic plan to bring commercial banking back to the branch.

COMMUNICATION
- Established the division's quarterly newsletter for distribution to the staff and volunteers of the Olympic sports organizations, which significantly improved communication and compliance with grant guidelines.
- Facilitated communication between developers and users; improved relationships by prioritizing IT changes and setting realistic user expectations.

COMPUTERS
- As a system administrator, improved SMU's computer network efficiency by identifying areas requiring change and developing, testing, and implementing new practices and procedures.
- Streamlined an automated network-based database that maintained records in excess of $1.3 million within the External Relations Office.
- Created and maintained Web pages to improve executive relationships for the Dean's Council.
- Championed the first-generation informational web site linked to major vendors and industry trade associations. Instrumental in the creation of the second-generation web site offering an e-commerce component—the first in the textile converting industry (www.tapetex.com).
- Maintained computer network support levels despite a $1.2 million budget cut.
- Decreased paperwork 50% by completely reviewing the circuit provisioning program.
- Opened an interactive CAD-CAM design studio used by customers to develop custom patterns and designs—the only one of its kind in the industry.

CONSTRUCTION
- Executed take-offs from blueprints, estimated costs, and bid jobs to ensure profitability.

CUSTOMER SERVICE
- Interviewed all company departments and created a process flow map for service delivery that eliminated redundancies and improved overall efficiency.
- Provided a high level of customer service to patients and their families.

- Proactively maintained client relationships with 300+ corporate accounts.
- Created a quick response customer service team equipped with contact management software.
- Developed a new specialist concept for providing customer technical service and provisioning of MCI's services that increased revenue by 40%.

EDUCATION ADMINISTRATION

- Selected to turn around a high school with declining enrollment, low teacher morale, a high dropout rate, deteriorating building, and poor academic reputation.
- Succeeded in revitalizing the staff and building consensus among teachers, the community, and students.
- Created a safe, productive, caring, and positive school climate through effective leadership that included modeling, rewards, communication, increased visibility, and appreciation for diversity.
- Developed and implemented innovative programs that have made Mitchell High School a magnet in the district.
- Implemented a variety of intervention programs to promote student achievement and retention.
- Improved attendance three percentage points by increasing the visibility of security personnel and creating an Attendance Committee that revised policies and improved parental involvement.
- Established an emphasis on instruction and ensured that all students were academically challenged and individually successful.
- Developed better programs and course offerings that resulted in the highest ACT improvement of any large high school on the Front Range.
- Improved writing scores on the DWA state assessments by an entire grade level.
- Achieved the highest scholarship dollar amount per graduate of any school in the district for 1999 – 2000.
- Recognized twice by the Chamber of Commerce for excellence in community partnerships.
- Partnered with Booz-Allen Hamilton, ARINC, WorldCom, and the Citadel Mall to adopt classes. Employees followed the students through all four years of high school, providing mentoring, career exploration, and training opportunities. Received the Colorado CAPE Award for the Booz-Allen Hamilton partnership.
- Developed a unique partnership with Peterson Air Force Base to enhance the Career Technology Center.
- Created an award-winning mentorship program with the Colorado Springs Firefighters Association that involves local firefighters mentoring at-risk students.
- Developed community partnerships to rehabilitate the physical plant using volunteer help and donated materials, which has generated a new sense of pride among students.
- Led the development of a courtroom building that provides classroom space for pre-law courses, mock trial competitions, and simulations of actual court cases.
- Implemented a pilot mentorship program called "Choices" to teach junior and senior student leaders how to mentor freshmen classmates toward improved performance.
- Developed a partnership with the El Paso County building and construction industry to provide hands-on experience for students interested in the trade.
- Approached the El Paso County Contractors Association for grants and sponsorships for the Wheels of Learning program, which prepares students for careers in the building trades.

EVENT PLANNING

- Developed a wide network of vendors, facilities, speakers, and caterers to meet specific needs.
- Revitalized underperforming programs and achieved significant profitability.
- As an Executive Officer to an Army General, managed more than 35 worldwide trips in 12 months.
- Assisted the director of development with special events, notably the 25th Anniversary Gala, which was the single most profitable event in the organization's history.

FIELD ENGINEER

- Technical expert called in to resolve the most difficult problems.
- Improved efficiency and lowered labor/job costs, significantly improving profitability.
- Implemented an engineering approach to problem identification and achieved a defect density rating of 1.9 when the industry standard is 1.4 and perfection is 2.0.

FINANCE

- Successfully guided the company through a lengthy period of extreme financial distress.
- Represented the company during the preparation of the first registered Internet public venture capital offering as well as several private placements.
- Conceived a stabilization plan to reduce deficits inherited from previous management and negotiated forgiveness of significant vendor debt.

FUND RAISING

- Raised $45,000 in three weeks for a heart transplant patient through newspaper, television, and radio promotion; set up bank accounts and coordinated special events.
- Provided information that helped one client reduce fund-raising costs by 65%.
- Founded a successful consulting business that provided fund-raising and development services to high-profile nonprofit organizations in New York and Colorado for more than twelve years. Developed a results-oriented reputation that ensured frequent referrals and repeat business from satisfied clients.
- One of three founders of a nonprofit theater venture that produced a three-week Equity showcase on Theatre Row, a premier Off-Broadway venue.
- Wrote and negotiated an umbrella agreement with an existing nonprofit organization to facilitate fundraising.
- Succeeded in raising enough funds to meet budget requirements when the norm in the industry is a loss.
- Solicited government, foundation, corporate, and individual contributions accounting for 32% of the $1.2 million operating budget.
- Formalized the fundraising program that is still used today. This established a sound financial foundation and provided the means for the organization to redefine itself amongst its peers as a premier instrument for promoting new playwrights.
- Created an all-purpose appeal that articulated the organization's history, mission, and programs.
- Part of a development team that raised $670,000—an 11% increase over the previous year—and exceeded corporate, foundation, and individual contribution goals.
- Researched and wrote grant proposals for foundation and corporate donors, generating an average of 20 grants per month to identified prospects.

GREENSKEEPER

- Gained extensive experience in growing and managing cool-season grasses, including knowledge of bentgrass greens, microclimatic conditions, and winterization.
- Enhanced turf grass quality and course playability using both current and innovative methods and technologies.

HEALTHCARE

- Part of the team responsible for the preparations that earned a score of 94 on the September 2002 JCAHO survey.
- Expanded the client base to include other Mercy subsidiaries, other hospitals, and various physician practices.

HOSPITALITY/TOURISM

- Built the hotel into a strong competitor for the city's business market and ranked in the top 10% for customer service out of 1,140 Hampton hotels.
- Developed housekeeping policies and procedures that resulted in a hotel cleanliness yield that exceeded corporate averages by as much as 23 points.
- Analyzed sales trends, developed forecasts and budgets, and set up rate structures that increased the average daily rate by $2.00 and occupancy by 1.7%.
- Promoted through the ranks from busboy to head waiter; developed a reputation for reliability and hard work; worked 35–40 hours per week while in college full-time.
- Inherited mother's restaurant specializing in casual lunch and catering; succeeded in growing the corporate client base and sold the business at a profit two years later.
- Maintained expenses below budget through accurate planning, purchasing, and waste reduction controls.
- Implemented operating efficiencies that kept the business profitable in spite of tight margins.
- Managed a restaurant and lounge recognized as first out of 54 in a five-state region.

HUMAN RESOURCES

- Designed and managed the company's self-funded hospitalization program, with resulting per-employee costs significantly below national averages.
- Created and implemented a progressive operations manual that significantly improved operating efficiency and, ultimately, profitability.
- Studied problematic behavioral trends, developed crisis intervention strategies and emergency responses, and made recommendations for changes to senior management.
- Conceptualized, developed, and co-facilitated The Silent Retreat, an award-winning experiential weekend for students and staff.
- Transformed the organizational culture and improved operating efficiency through cross-functional coaching/training and tactical restructuring that decentralized operations and brought the employees closer to their tasks and clients.
- Instituted a sales group compensation program that was completely performance based, motivating a 10% increase in sales.
- Developed a measurement process to analyze on-time and complete delivery performance, which permitted rapid corrective actions and improved response rates.
- Provided behavioral feedback as an executive coach to the group leaders and regional presidents.

- Created an atmosphere that valued continual learning, risk taking, and personal accountability among employees.
- Improved productivity and morale by initiating systems for accountability, formalizing job duties, and instituting training programs.

INVENTORY MANAGEMENT AND LOGISTICS
- Achieved a 98.8% service goal with 17.9 inventory turns in the grocery warehouse, where the corporate benchmark is 97% with 18 turns.
- Collaborated with category managers, marketing department, 113 vendors, and transportation providers to create supply and logistics cost-saving opportunities and to coordinate direct store deliveries.
- Helped save the Lane & Edson account by providing support for a critical shipping problem.
- Authored new interim and year-end physical inventory procedures for increased efficiency in the annual external audit.
- Improved warehouse requisition and receipt processing to less than one day; location accuracy to 98%; inventory accuracy to 97%; demand satisfaction rates to 90%; and zero balance rates to 3.6% (reduced from 36%).
- Re-engineered existing supply processes to save limited resources, recovering $26 million.
- Received the Joint Service Commendation Award for improving inventory stock levels, accountability, consumption tracking, restocking, and customs procedures for the joint U.S. task force of Army, Navy, Air Force, and Marines.
- Honored with two Meritorious Service Medals for innovations in logistical support.

JOINT VENTURES
- Approached a Belgian mill and formed a partnership that permits CTM to serve as their agent in the U.S., generating $2 million in new annual revenue.
- Created a strategic alliance with a major distributor of raw materials to the footwear industry, opening new Asian markets for the company and creating significant additional profit centers.
- Established a strategic distribution partnership in Latin America with Glen Raven Mexicana that expanded the market globally.
- Negotiated exclusive North American distribution agreements with two European mills, resulting in an annual sales increase of approximately $3 million.
- Developed a strategic partnership with Milliken, Inc., and Duro Industries to better serve one of the company's largest customers, W. L. Gore, resulting in a 350% increase in revenue over three years.

LAW
- Successfully negotiated individual product liability settlements of up to $250,000.
- Member of a three-attorney panel appointed by the New Mexico Court of Appeals to issue advisory decisions in pending civil appeals.
- Wrote the advisory decision in the appeal of *Miller v. NM Dept. of Transportation,* the essence of which was adopted by the New Mexico Supreme Court.
- Selected twice in fifteen months as an arbitrator for the New Mexico trial-level court to arbitrate cases with damage claims less than $15,000, using procedures similar to those governing American Arbitration Association proceedings.
- Lead counsel or sole counsel for the injured plaintiff / worker in at least 30 jury trials with a minimum trial length of three days, plus another 50 non-jury trials of at least two days.

- Since 1983, have prepared and prosecuted to conclusion, either by trial or settlement, over 650 workers' compensation cases involving both physical and economic injuries.
- Met deadlines for pretrial procedures, trials, and appellate briefings by effectively utilizing attorney associates and support staff.
- Designed a complete set of recurring forms to manage a typical workers' compensation claim from initial client interview through requested findings and conclusions.

MARKETING
- Developed a vital network of business and industry contacts instrumental to the rapid growth of the company.
- Successfully gained new customers through effective marketing, sales presentations, and follow-up.
- As marketing director for a retirement home, increased occupancy rates from 20% to 90%.
- Changed the company's perception in the marketplace by creating innovative marketing materials and making it more visible.
- Managed the company's transition to a global marketing focus through targeted sales planning, re-engineering of operations, and sound financial management, leading to sales diversification and enhanced opportunities for future growth in a shrinking market.
- Developed proprietary products for customers that strengthened their brand name equity and increased the company's profit margins.
- Enhanced domestic representation and diversified the product lines, increasing sales by 40% to $36 million.
- Developed and conducted quarterly focus groups with up to 150 management users; provided executive management with formal feedback that included solution-driven results.
- Developed effective sales and marketing programs that included direct mail campaigns, print advertising, promotions, and free delivery services.
- Wrote a strategic operating plan to improve profitability by more effectively allocating resources to key market segments and deploying technology to increase efficiency.

MANUFACTURING
- Increased equipment availability from 78% to 94% within the first month by reducing down time through the implementation of a quality improvement strategy.
- Reduced maintenance work-in-process to less than 90 days with a production index of >1.0.
- Designed and implemented new floor layout to improve efficiencies and work flow.
- Reduced labor standards by an average of 25% on all product lines.
- Reduced rework rate by 50% by detailed in-process inspection.
- Reduced monthly failure rate from 2.5 units to .30 units.
- Implemented quick responses to assembly line accidents and other emergencies.

MERGERS & ACQUISITIONS
- Member of the Wells Fargo corporate steering committee responsible for merging the operations of the two banks (Norwest and Wells Fargo) into a functional sales tracking system.
- Coordinated the merger of a bank into one location and assumed the management of a new bank gained in the acquisition.

MILITARY

- Consistently promoted ahead of peers; selected for Technical Sergeant under the Stripes for Exceptional Performers (STEP) program.
- Selected for the 1992 Noncommissioned Officer of the Year Award at the command level.
- Successfully managed the maintenance of automotive equipment returning from Desert Storm, taking on twice the normal workload with no additional assets.

NURSING

- Member of the Access collaborative department team; helped to coordinate changes that improved patient satisfaction by allowing patients immediate access to the provider of their choice at times convenient for them.
- Ensured laboratory protocol was in compliance with Clinical Laboratory Improvement Amendment (CLIA).
- Coordinated a full 80-victim disaster drill and then rewrote the entire disaster plan in collaboration with the staff development RN.
- Furnished high-quality nursing care in the emergency room of a regional hospital seeing 4,000 patients per month, 600 requiring pediatric care.
- Instituted a Braslowe Tape System of acute pediatric assessment and treatment, as well as a geriatric fall prevention and risk assessment program.
- Designed and implemented a tool to identify victims of domestic violence who presented to the ER, which ensured proper care and follow-up.
- Ensured optimum patient care in spite of often adversarial relationships between private and public emergency services.
- Initiated and participated in staff and interdisciplinary team conferences to improve the quality of care delivered to residents.
- Served as a role model for county public health nurses and other providers.
- Acted as a resource person to new nursing staff and facilitated team cohesion.

QUALITY ASSURANCE

- Investigated and resolved quality and service complaints, promoting repeat business and improving profitability.
- Honored for a commitment to 100% customer satisfaction and zero defects.
- Improved response to system outages by streamlining procedures and keeping leadership informed.

SALES

- Referred more than $15 million in new placements annually.
- Recognized by Lanier's Atlanta headquarters for generating the highest yearly sales volume in the Western Region during the first six months on the job; eight-time recipient of the monthly top production award.
- Hired geographically dispersed sales executives and developed a team-based environment that communicates horizontally and not just vertically.
- Researched and implemented a Web-based software tool (salesforce.com) to enhance sales reporting from the field.
- Expanded the sales force to facilitate the development of high-profile key accounts, growing sales from $35 to $54 million.

- Designed sales management processes to promote sales effectiveness and achieve long-term revenue growth and increase customer loyalty across multiple channels.
- Created solid working relationships with internal and external partners to improve opportunity identification and sales closings.
- Selected for several corporate task forces, including retail job descriptions, retail incentives, and go-forward sales training curriculum initiatives.
- Selected as a statewide sales trainer to introduce and implement an innovative sales process long before the industry moved in that direction.
- Increased gross sales from $1,500 to $80,000 per month in one year.
- Interfaced with vendors, customer service representatives, and medical personnel to streamline product delivery and maintained effective working relationships.
- Utilized negotiation and persuasion skills to gain a continually higher percentage of sales per account.
- Influenced the group's senior leadership to support and participate in a defined sales management accountability matrix that promoted active supervision of operations that drive results.
- Completed month-long corporate training program in Manhattan and succeeded in developing 200 clients in the first year with $4.3 million in assets.

SECRETARY, CLERK
- Displayed a professional demeanor with a cheerful positive attitude.
- Took reservations for a private beach and minimized conflicts in the schedule.
- Improved access to treatment options by developing a resource information sheet for drug treatment centers, respite options, and other resources in Colorado Springs and Denver which was adopted by multiple centers statewide.

TEACHER
- Prepared a master plan for student accountability as chairperson of the Proficiency Committee.
- Selected to assist in the evaluation, modification, and organization of Cheraw Elementary School's math, science, reading, and writing curriculum.
- Developed a successful classroom motivational tool that included special shirts for students.
- Wrote multiple grants and received funding for special programs.
- Awarded "Outstanding American History Teacher of the Year" for Southeast Colorado by the Daughters of the American Revolution (1997).
- Appointed to the Master Teacher Advisory Group for the U.S. Space Foundation (1997).
- Selected for the national "Time Magazine Award" for developing and implementing a mock presidential election for all of the schools in the Cheraw District (1988).
- Recipient of a Colorado Endowment for the Humanities (1993).

TELECOMMUNICATION
- Identified 180 leased communication circuits for removal, saving $2.1 million in annual leased line costs.
- Researched and developed a communications network strategy for U.S. locations in the Netherlands, saving $480,000 in international leased line costs and ensuring survivability of communications services.

TRAINING

- Coached training staff to improve the quality of seminar presentations.
- Taught six weeks of initial management training and three weeks of continued management training at The Management Training Center; personally responsible for launching the careers of 400 management employees.
- Redesigned and implemented a new training model based on the Mager Method for the annual ten-day resident advisor training program, which is still in use today.
- Introduced a sales training program that included 18 months of in-house experience prior to being assigned to a designated territory.
- Developed cross-training programs that improved the morale and the efficiency of operations and lowered turnover rates.

Awards and Honors

In a research study of corporate hiring practices sponsored by Career Masters Institute *(www.cmi.com),* the researcher found that decision makers weren't much interested in awards even if they applied to the job they were trying to fill.

The study concluded that "hiring managers don't know how to judge the value of awards. For example, a résumé that just mentions the name of the award might not provide enough information. However, readers would learn more if they knew this award went only to the top five performers in a sales force numbering more than five hundred."

The key, then, is to focus on the accomplishment more than the award itself. Naming the honor or award is secondary to the return on investment the hiring manager perceives from the sentence. For example:

- Received the National Sales Excellence Award in 2000 by becoming one of the top five producers of mutual fund sales within the peer group.

- Selected by United Technologies Sikorsky Aircraft Company to receive their Igor I. Sikorsky Helicopter Rescue Award for a successful high-risk mountain rescue.

- Won two quarterly superior customer service awards in two years by competing with 18 bakeries in the district.

- Selected for the Service Excellence Award (4th quarter of 2000) for personal customer service excellence.

- Received a monetary award for improving the working relationship between couriers and service agents.

- Achieved Best-in-Class customer service scores based on quarterly client surveys.

- Recipient of the Gold Level Reward for exceptional performance during 2000.

- Received Gold Star award for exceptional performance during a crisis call.

Remember the rule that there is an exception to every rule in the résumé business? Well, here's another one. If the award is so self-explanatory in your industry that explaining it would be insulting to your reader, then list those awards or honors in a separate section at the bottom of your résumé, like this for a teacher:

- High Plains Educator Award (2001)
- Who's Who Among America's Teachers (1999, 2000)
- Outstanding Young Woman of America (2003)

. . . or like this for an Olympic medalist in Taekwondo:

- Awarded the USOC Developmental Coach of the Year, Taekwondo (1996)
- Olympic Games, Bronze Medal (1988), selected as captain of the team
- Taekwondo Times Hall of Fame (1988)
- Pan American Games, Bronze Medal (1987)
- Pan Am Taekwondo championships, Gold Medal (1980, 1986)
- U.S. Olympic Festival, Gold Medal (1986)
- World Games, Silver Medal (1985), U.S. World Team Member (8 times)
- World Championships, Bronze Medal (1983, 1985, 1987)
- Selected as an International Referee by the World Taekwondo Federation
- Captain, U.S. National Team (1983 – 1988)
- President's Best Player Award (1983)

Chapter 8

Now that you have the words on paper, go back to each list and think about which items are relevant to your current job target. Cross out those things that don't relate, including entire jobs (like flipping hamburgers back in high school if you are now an electrical engineer with ten years of experience).

Remember, your résumé is just an enticer, a way to get your foot in the door. It isn't intended to be all-inclusive. You can choose to go back only as far as your jobs relate to your present objective. Be careful not to delete sentences that contain the most important keywords you identified in Step 4.

Change Is Inevitable

You know the old saying, "The only constant is change." Perhaps you should make a copy of the pages before you begin marking them up. They are a great record of your work history, and you never know when you might want to change careers, which means you would need some of that information.

According to the U.S. Department of Labor, the average worker today will change jobs 15 times in his or her career and hold 9.2 jobs between the ages of 18 and 34. Today, workers are much more free to change not just jobs but careers.

I have been writing résumés since 1980, and the biggest change I've seen since the early 90s is the number of clients who have decided to, for example, leave computer programming for acting or to change from nursing to pharmaceutical sales.

Part of the reason for this transition is social and part is the result of the modern workplace. According to William Hine, Dean of the School of Adult and Continuing Education at Eastern Illinois University, "The half-life of a college degree is three to five years." There was a time when you could graduate from college and stay in the

> The average worker today will change jobs 15 times.

same job for thirty years and then retire with a gold watch. Not so today. You must be committed to lifelong learning or your career will leave you behind.

That means you can also make the choice to retool, get a new degree, and start a new career in mid-life. It's perfectly acceptable.

It also means that being a packrat can pay off when you decide to change careers! So, store the original sheets in the same file you created for your performance evaluations and job descriptions, and use the copies for this step.

Take the copies and decide which jobs are relevant to today's job search. You only need to use about 10 to 15 years of those jobs, unless there is something very powerful in your early career that will help you get a job. Now, set aside the jobs that are too old or irrelevant. Try to limit your list of final jobs to no more than six, although you can list more if they are truly relevant or contain valuable experience.

Focus on the sentences in the relevant experience summaries.

- Which ones are the most powerful?
- Which ones summarize your experience the best?
- Which ones contain the keywords of your industry?
- Which ones highlight your accomplishments the best?

Delete Education

Next, do the same for your education and training worksheets. Copy them, file away the originals, and cross out anything that doesn't relate to your current job goal.

That does not apply to your formal education, however. Even if you have a graduate degree in your career field and your undergraduate degree is unrelated, leave them both on your résumé. Your reader will need to see the progression of your formal education.

If you have a bachelor's degree and an associate degree, you don't need to list them both unless there is something about the major of your associate degree that you don't have in your bachelor's degree. Remember, it is okay to list almost anything on your résumé as long as it is relevant to your job search.

Chapter 9

It's time to do some serious writing now. You must make dynamic, attention-getting sentences of the duties and accomplishments you have listed under each job, combining related items to avoid short choppy phrases. Here are the secrets to great résumé sentences:

- In résumés, you never use personal pronouns (I, my, me). Instead of saying: "*I planned, organized, and directed the timely and accurate production of code products with estimated annual revenues of $1 million*" you should say: "*Planned, organized, and directed. . . .*" Writing in the first person makes your sentences more powerful and attention grabbing, but using personal pronouns throughout a résumé is awkward. Your reader will assume that you are referring to yourself, so the personal pronouns can be avoided.

- Make your sentences positive, brief, and accurate. Since your ultimate goal is to get a human being to read your résumé, remember to structure the sentences so they are interesting to read.

- Use verbs at the beginning of each sentence (designed, supervised, managed, developed, formulated, and so on) to make them more powerful (see the list at the end of this chapter).

- Incorporate keywords from the list you made in Step 4 (Chapter 5).

- Make certain each word means something and contributes to the quality of the sentence.

Finding Help

If it is difficult for you to write clear, concise sentences, take the information you have just listed to a professional writer who can help you turn it into a winning résumé. Choose someone who is a Nationally Certified Résumé Writer

> *Make certain each word means something and contributes to the quality of the sentence.*

(NCRW) or Certified Professional Résumé Writer (CPRW). That way you can be assured that the person has passed the strictest tests of résumé writing and design in the country, including peer review, administered by the National Résumé Writers' Association (NRWA) and Professional Association of Résumé Writers (PARW).

To find certified résumé writers, check these web sites:

- National Résumé Writers' Association: *www.nrwa.com*
- Professional Association of Résumé Writers: *www.parw.com*
- Career Masters Institute: *www.cmi.com*
- Professional Résumé Writing and Research Association: *www.prwra. com*
- Certified Résumé Writers Guild: *www.certifiedresumewritersguild.com*
- Certified Résumé Writers: *www.certifiedresumewriters.net*

What are the benefits of partnering with a professional résumé writer? According to the NRWA, you will gain access to:

- Expert résumé writing, editing, and design skills.

- Needed objectivity and expertise to play up your strengths, downplay your weaknesses, and position yourself for interview success.

- The precise know-how to target your career and industry correctly.

- Winning résumé, job search, interviewing, and salary negotiation strategies from recognized experts.

- Experienced professionals who have passed rigorous résumé industry exams and demonstrated their commitment to the profession by obtaining ongoing training.

Résumé writers work in one of two ways: 1) they gather all of the information they need from you in a personal interview, 2) they require that you complete a long questionnaire before they begin working on your résumé, or 3) they use a combination of both methods. In any case, you have already done most of the data collection if you have followed Steps 1 through 6 and Steps 10 and 11 in this book. This preparation sometimes makes the résumé easier to write and many professional résumé writers will pass on that savings to you in the form of lower fees.

If you are going to proceed from here and finish the résumé on your own, let me show you how to rewrite sentences so they are more powerful. The original sentences in these examples were on real résumés. The rewrites are my fine-tuning based on interviews with each client, which gathered more information and clarified the original intent of the writer.

Original Sentence: Responsible for leading team of application engineers, delivery consultants, and technical trainers in pre-sales and post-sales activities.

Rewrite: Led a team of 20 application engineers, delivery consultants, and technical trainers in the development of customized enterprise software solutions.

Original Sentence: Generation of accurate and meaningful client proposals based on initial client needs and assessment.

Rewrite: Generated effective client proposals based on a comprehensive assessment of client requirements.

Original Sentence: Telecommunication sales associate who achieved quota each month after training phase.

Rewrite: Successfully sold telecommunication services, achieving sales goals each month and generated more than $1 million in annual revenue.

Original Sentence: Responsible to ensure that time is spent on being pro-active about the future financial needs of the district.

Rewrite: Proactive in ensuring that the future financial needs of the district were met.

Original Sentence: Helped the district make assessment and accountability that accompanies data not an event but rather a practice that we seek and value.

Rewrite: Assured that assessment and accountability became part of the district's culture and not a simple event.

Original Sentence: Marketing Coordinator; for all internal and external marketing for Club Sports six up-scale fitness clubs and a hotel and fitness resort.

Rewrite: Coordinated all of the internal and external marketing for six upscale fitness clubs and the Renaissance ClubSport hotel and fitness resort.

Original Sentence: Inside sale support responsible for aftermarket parts and equipment sales for over 200 municipalities as well as expediting and tracking purchase orders, sales generated yearly were approximately $100,000.

Rewrite: Provided inside sales support for aftermarket parts and equipment sales to 200+ municipalities, personally generating annual sales of more than $100,000.

Original Sentence: Processed and reviewed applications for residency.

Rewrite: Reviewed applications for residency, checked credit and personal references, and approved new occupants.

Original Sentence: Sold and achieved sales goals.

Rewrite: Integral member of the teller team responsible for exceeding sales goals for credit card accounts, ATM cards, instant cash cards, and new account referrals.

Original Sentence: Coordinating with the local printer, all collateral for the club.

Rewrite: Developed collateral materials and ensured that all clubs had the most recent sales aids.

Power Verbs

Now that you have some samples of good writing, let's look at the words that made it possible. Power verbs at the beginning of sentences make them more interesting and, well, "powerful." Try to use a variety of these words. It's easy to choose the same one to begin every sentence, but there are synonyms buried within this list that will make your writing better.

A

abated
abbreviated
abolished
abridged
absolved
absorbed
accelerated
accentuated
accommodated
accompanied
accomplished
accounted for
accrued
accumulated
achieved
acquired
acted
activated
actuated
adapted
added
addressed
adhered to
adjusted
administered
adopted
advanced
advertised
advised
advocated
affirmed
aided
alerted
aligned
allayed
alleviated

allocated
allotted
altered
amassed
amended
amplified
analyzed
answered
anticipated
appeased
applied
appointed
appraised
approached
appropriated
approved
arbitrated
aroused
arranged
articulated
ascertained
aspired
assembled
assessed
assigned
assimilated
assisted
assumed
assured
attained
attended
attracted
audited
augmented
authored
authorized
automated
averted

avoided
awarded

B

balanced
bargained
began
benchmarked
benefitted
bid
billed
blended
blocked
bolstered
boosted
bought
branded
bridged
broadened
brought
budgeted
built

C

calculated
calibrated
canvassed
capitalized
captured
cared for
carried
carried out
carved
catalogued
categorized
caught

cautioned
cemented
centralized
certified
chaired
challenged
championed
changed
channeled
charged
charted
checked
chose
chronicled
circulated
circumvented
cited
clarified
classified
cleaned
cleared
closed
coached
co-authored
coded
cold called
collaborated
collated
collected
combined
commanded
commenced
commended
commissioned
communicated
compared
competed
compiled

complemented
completed
complied
composed
compounded
computed
conceived
concentrated
conceptualized
concluded
condensed
conducted
conferred
configured
confirmed
confronted
connected
conserved
considered
consolidated
constructed
consulted
consummated
contacted
continued
contracted
contributed
controlled
converted
conveyed
convinced
cooperated
coordinated
copied
corrected
correlated
corresponded
counseled
counted
created
credited with
critiqued
cultivated
customized
cut

D

dealt
debated
debugged
decentralized
decided
decoded
decreased
dedicated
deferred
defined
delegated
deleted
delineated
delivered
demonstrated
deployed
depreciated
derived
described
designated
designed
detailed
detected
determined
developed
devised
devoted
diagnosed
diagramed
differentiated
diffused
directed
disbursed
disclosed
discounted
discovered
discussed
dispatched
dispensed
dispersed
displayed
disposed
disproved

dissected
disseminated
dissolved
distinguished
distributed
diversified
diverted
divested
divided
documented
doubled
drafted
dramatized
drew up
drove

E

earned
eased
economized
edited
educated
effected
elaborated
elected
elevated
elicited
eliminated
embraced
emphasized
employed
empowered
enabled
encountered
encouraged
ended
endorsed
enforced
engaged
engineered
enhanced
enlarged
enlisted
enriched

enrolled
ensured
entered
entertained
enticed
equipped
established
estimated
evaluated
examined
exceeded
exchanged
executed
exercised
exhibited
expanded
expedited
experienced
experimented
explained
explored
exposed
expressed
extended
extracted
extrapolated

F

fabricated
facilitated
factored
familiarized
fashioned
fielded
filed
filled
finalized
financed
fine-tuned
finished
fixed
focused
followed
forecasted

forged
formalized
formatted
formed
formulated
fortified
forwarded
fostered
fought
found
founded
framed
fulfilled
functioned as
funded
furnished
furthered

G

gained
garnered
gathered
gauged
gave
generated
governed
graded
graduated
granted
graphed
grasped
greeted
grew
grouped
guaranteed
guided

H

halted
halved
handled
headed
heightened

held
helped
hired
honed
hosted
hypnotized
hypothesized

I

identified
ignited
illuminated
illustrated
implemented
imported
improved
improvised
inaugurated
incited
included
incorporated
increased
incurred
indicated
individualized
indoctrinated
induced
influenced
informed
infused
initialized
initiated
innovated
inspected
inspired
installed
instigated
instilled
instituted
instructed
insured
integrated
intensified

interacted
interceded
interfaced
interpreted
intervened
interviewed
introduced
invented
inventoried
invested
investigated
invigorated
invited
involved
isolated
issued
itemized

J

joined
judged
justified

L

launched
learned
leased
lectured
led
lessened
leveraged
licensed
lifted
lightened
limited
linked
liquidated
listened
litigated
loaded
lobbied
localized
located
logged

M

made
maintained
managed
mandated
maneuvered
manipulated
manufactured
mapped
marked
marketed
mastered
maximized
measured
mediated
memorized
mentored
merchandised
merged
merited
met
minimized
mobilized
modeled
moderated
modernized
modified
molded
monitored
monopolized
motivated
mounted
moved
multiplied

N

named
narrated
navigated
negotiated
netted
networked
neutralized
nominated
normalized

noticed
notified
nurtured

O

observed
obtained
offered
officiated
offset
opened
operated
optimized
orchestrated
ordered
organized
oriented
originated
outdistanced
outlined
outperformed
overcame
overhauled
oversaw
owned

P

paced
packaged
packed
paid
pared
participated
partnered
passed
patterned
penalized
penetrated
perceived
perfected
performed
permitted
persuaded

phased out
photographed
piloted
pinpointed
pioneered
placed
planned
played
polled
posted
praised
predicted
prepared
prescribed
presented
preserved
presided
prevailed
prevented
priced
printed
prioritized
probed
processed
procured
produced
profiled
programmed
progressed
projected
promoted
prompted
proofread
proposed
protected
proved
provided
pruned
publicized
published
purchased
pursued

Q

quadrupled
qualified
quantified
queried
questioned
quoted

R

raised
rallied
ranked
rated
reached
reacted
read
realigned
realized
rearranged
reasoned
rebuilt
received
reclaimed
recognized
recommended
reconciled
reconstructed
recorded
recovered
recruited
rectified
redesigned
redirected
reduced
re-engineered
referred
refined
refocused
regained
registered
regulated

rehabilitated
reinforced
reinstated
reiterated
rejected
related
released
relied
relieved
remained
remediated
remodeled
rendered
renegotiated
renewed
reorganized
repaired
replaced
replicated
replied
reported
represented
reproduced
requested
required
requisitioned
researched
reserved
reshaped
resolved
responded
restored
restructured
retained
retooled
retrieved
returned
revamped
revealed
reversed
reviewed
revised
revitalized
revolutionized

rewarded
risked
rotated
routed

safeguarded
salvaged
saved
scanned
scheduled
screened
sculptured
searched
secured
segmented
seized
selected
sent
separated
sequenced
served as
serviced
settled
set up
shaped
shared
sharpened
shipped
shortened
showed
shrank
signed
simplified
simulated
sketched
skilled
slashed
smoothed
sold
solicited
solidified

solved
sorted
sourced
sparked
spearheaded
specialized
specified
speculated
spent
spoke
sponsored
spread
spurred
stabilized
staffed
staged
standardized
started
steered
stimulated
strategized
streamlined
strengthened
stressed
stretched
structured
studied
subcontracted
submitted
substantiated
substituted
succeeded
suggested
summarized
superceded
supervised
supplied
supported
surpassed
surveyed
swayed
swept

symbolized
synchronized
synthesized
systemized

tabulated
tackled
tailored
talked
tallied
targeted
tasted
taught
teamed
tempered
tended
terminated
tested
testified
tied
tightened
took
topped
totaled
traced
tracked
traded
trained
transacted
transcribed
transferred
transformed
transitioned
translated
transmitted
transported
traveled
treated
trimmed
tripled
troubleshot
turned
tutored
typed

U

uncovered
underlined
underscored
undertook
underwrote
unearthed
unified
united
updated
upgraded
upheld
urged
used
utilized

V

validated
valued
vaulted
verbalized
verified
viewed
visited
visualized
voiced
volunteered

W

weathered
weighed
welcomed
widened
withstood
witnessed
won
worked
wove
wrote

Y

yielded

You are almost done! Now, go back to the sentences you have written and think about their order of presentation. Put a number 1 by the most important description of what you did for each job. Then place a number 2 by the next most important duty or accomplishment, and so on until you have numbered each sentence.

Again, think logically and from the perspective of a potential employer. Keep related items together so the reader doesn't jump from one concept to another. Make the thoughts flow smoothly.

The first sentence in a job description is usually an overall statement of the position's major responsibilities. The rest of the sentences should begin with your most important duties and accomplishments and proceed to lesser ones.

Let me give you an example of a job description in rough draft format and one that has been rearranged, and I'm sure you will see what I mean.

JOHNSON UNIVERSITY HOSPITAL, New Brunswick, New Jersey (2000 – 2003)
Director, Pediatric Emergency Department
- Recently developed and implemented an expansion of the department into a new children's hospital.
- Hired and managed a staff of 40 employees, directed performance improvement initiatives, and implemented departmental standards of care.
- Analyzed trends for key indicators to improve subsequent code responses.
- Member of the Performance Improvement Committee.
- Analyzed 72-hour readmission trends to find problems with practice patterns.
- Selected for the Code Response Team: Developed a new performance improvement form.
- Redesigned resuscitation guidelines for residents and nursing staff.
- Directed clinical and administrative operations of a 12,000-visit-per-year pediatric emergency department.
- Developed and managed an operating budget of $1.3 million.

> *The first sentence in a job description is usually an overall statement of the job's major responsibilities.*

- Developed staffing standards and evaluated the qualifications/competence of department personnel to provide appropriate levels of patient care.
- Member of the Health Policy and Strategic Planning Committee responsible for preparing the hospital and staff for JCAHO accreditation reviews.
- Implemented a pain initiative.

After numbering and rearranging the sentences, the section reads much stronger and has a better flow.

JOHNSON UNIVERSITY HOSPITAL, New Brunswick, New Jersey (2000 – 2003)
Director, Pediatric Emergency Department
- Directed clinical and administrative operations of a 12,000-visit-per-year pediatric emergency department.
- Developed and managed an operating budget of $1.3 million.
- Hired and managed a staff of 40 employees, directed performance improvement initiatives, and implemented departmental standards of care.
- Developed staffing standards and evaluated the qualifications/competence of department personnel to provide appropriate levels of patient care.
- Member of the Health Policy and Strategic Planning Committee responsible for preparing the hospital and staff for JCAHO accreditation reviews.

Key Accomplishments:
- Recently developed and implemented an expansion of the department into a new children's hospital.
- Member of the Performance Improvement Committee: Analyzed 72-hour readmission trends to find problems with practice patterns. Implemented a pain initiative. Redesigned resuscitation guidelines for residents and nursing staff.
- Selected for the Code Response Team: Developed a new performance improvement form. Analyzed trends for key indicators to improve subsequent code responses.

Here is my reasoning for rearranging the sentences:

1. The first sentence was selected because it was a good overall statement of the job's major responsibility.

2. The second sentence added a further sense of scope by describing the size of the director's budget.

3. As did the third sentence by discussing the number of employees managed and other supervisory responsibilities.

4. The next two sentences are secondary job duties and special assignments.

5. In order to emphasize achievements, key accomplishments were pulled out into a separate section.

6. The first bullet was the most important accomplishment and the most recent.

7. All of the bullets that applied to the Performance Improvement Committee were listed together in a separate paragraph.

8. The last accomplishment was the least important.

Before and After Sample

Perhaps it would help to see a sample of a résumé before it had been rewritten and rearranged. The résumé on the next two pages was a first attempt without following the instructions in this book. The final version is shown on the last two pages of this chapter.

Pay special attention to the way bullets were expanded and rearranged to make them more powerful and compelling. The computer skills and education sections were moved to the top of the résumé because they were Paul's strongest qualifications for his new job goal (web site design).

PAUL O. JONES
1234 North Tejon Street
Denver, CO 80210

303.123.4567
Jones1234@pcisys.net

Objective	A challenging technical position at an excelling high tech company.
Education	**University of Colorado**, Colorado Springs Bachelor of Arts in Fine Arts Studio, December 2002 • Primary Emphasis: Digital Imaging, Sculpture

Professional Courses
- Intermediate HTML
- Advanced HTML
- Windows NT 4.0 Administration
- UNIX Fundamentals

Qualifications

Very attentive to accuracy and detail, as well as efficiency and organization. Excellent written, verbal, and interpersonal skills.

- Programming Languages: HTML, exposure to JavaScript.
- OS Platforms: Windows (9x/NT/2000/XP), exposure to MacOS and UNIX.
- Software: Adobe Photoshop, Adobe Image Ready, Microsoft Internet Information Server, WebTrends Analysis Suite, and Microsoft Office.

Experience

WorldCom, Inc.   **May 1998 – June 2002**
2424 Garden of the Gods Road • Colorado Springs, Colorado 80919

Software Development (Applications Developer II)
- Responsible for the design, development, and maintenance of several WorldCom intranet and internet web sites.
- Redesigned existing intranet and internet web sites inherited from other groups/organizations within WorldCom to provide users with a fresh browsing experience and enhanced organization of the web site content.

System Administrator (Software Systems Engineer I)
- Responsible for the implementation, monitoring, and maintenance of several WorldCom intranet and internet web sites and web servers within both Windows and UNIX environments.
- Provided weekly web traffic and usage analysis reports for many of the sites hosted within the Windows and UNIX web server environments using WebTrends Analysis Suite.

Best Buy Stores, Inc.   **August 1992 – April 1998**
801 North Academy Boulevard • Colorado Springs, Colorado 80909

Customer Service, Service Technician, and Sales
- Performed sales and return/exchange transactions, handled customer issues, and placed service orders.
- Performed testing/troubleshooting and minor repairs on consumer electronics, handled shipping, receiving, and inventory of repair units.
- Made sales in Media (software & music), Computer hardware and accessories, Cellular Phones, and Digital Satellite Systems.

86

Other Experience   ***The Mercury Cougar Collector's Page***   **Sep 1995 – Feb 1999**

Conception, design, and maintenance of an automotive web site, in which enthusiasts of the 1967-73 Mercury Cougar could display photos of their cars and obtain information.

Exhibitions and Awards

Student Art Exhibition

Gallery of Contemporary Art • University of Colorado, Colorado Springs

May 1998 – Sculpture
May 1997 – Sculpture
May 1996 – Digital Image

Aardvark-Zymurgy: The works of the '97-98 UCCS Art Graduates
December 1997

The Warehouse Gallery, Colorado Springs, Colorado

Display of two sculptures and a digital image.

***Purchase Prize*, Student Art Exhibition**   **May 1996**

Gallery of Contemporary Art • University of Colorado, Colorado Springs

Digital image, *Message from the Gods*, was purchased by the university for display in the University Center.

PAUL O. JONES

QUALIFICATIONS
- Creative Web Developer with a strong background in the design, development, and administration of large corporate Intranet and Internet web sites.
- Detail-oriented professional who gains great satisfaction from knowing that a project was done right.
- Enthusiastic team player with an outgoing, friendly communication style.

COMPUTER SKILLS

Programming Languages: HTML, MS Visual InterDev, JavaScript

Operating Systems: Windows (9x/NT/2000/XP), Macintosh, and UNIX

Design Software: Adobe Photoshop, Adobe Image Ready, Adobe Live Motion, Lightwave 3-D

Business Applications: MS Word, Excel, Access, PowerPoint, Outlook, Internet Explorer, Microsoft Internet Information Server, WebTrends Analysis Suite

EDUCATION

BACHELOR OF ARTS (December 2002)
University of Colorado, Colorado Springs, Colorado
- Major in Fine Arts Studio with an emphasis on digital imaging and sculpture
- Computer course work: Electronic Imaging, Advanced Project in Electronic Imaging, Web Art, Advanced Computer Art, Introduction to Computer Art
- Design course work: Independent Study in Fine Arts, Photography, 20th Century Sculpture, Advanced Drawing, Art History, Color Drawing, Advanced Studio Problems, Studio 3-D, Beginning Studio 2-D
- 3-D Topics: Form, Wood, Wood Sculpture, Advanced Sculpture, Advanced Figure Sculpture
- Business course work: Conflict Management, Macroeconomics, Interpersonal Communications, Political Science, Quantitative and Qualitative Reasoning Skills

PROFESSIONAL DEVELOPMENT
- Intermediate and Advanced HTML, WorldCom, Colorado Springs, Colorado
- Windows NT 4.0 Administration, WorldCom, Colorado Springs, Colorado
- UNIX Fundamentals, WorldCom, Colorado Springs, Colorado
- Lightwave 3-D Modeling Software, Washburn University, Denver, Colorado

EXPERIENCE

FREELANCE WEB DESIGNER (1995 – present)
Paul White Consulting, Colorado Springs, Colorado
- Designed a web site for High West Siding and Windows—www.highwestsiding.com. (2003)
- Conceived, designed and maintained a web site for enthusiasts of the 1967–1973 Mercury Cougar called The Mercury Cougar Collector's Page. The site allowed interested people to display photos of their classic cars and obtain information. (1995 – 1999)

APPLICATIONS DEVELOPER II (Software Developer) (1999 – 2002)
WorldCom, Colorado Springs, Colorado
- Designed, developed, and maintained several WorldCom Intranet and Internet web sites.
- Met with internal customers to determine their requirements, brainstormed with the development team, and designed the look and feel of each site.
- Redesigned existing web sites inherited from other groups and organizations within WorldCom to provide users with a fresh browsing experience and enhanced organization of content.
- Recognized for reliability, initiative, customer service skills, and ability to meet tight deadlines.
- Discovered a virus attack on the servers and recovered data quickly to minimize downtime.

ADDRESS
1234 N. Tejon Street • Denver, Colorado 80210
Phone: (303) 123-4567 • E-mail: jones1234@pcisys.net

EXPERIENCE **(continued)**	**SOFTWARE SYSTEMS ENGINEER I (System Administrator)** (1998 – 1999) **WorldCom**, Colorado Springs, Colorado

SOFTWARE SYSTEMS ENGINEER I (System Administrator) (1998 – 1999)
WorldCom, Colorado Springs, Colorado
- Served as primary systems administrator for 20 Windows NT servers and backup administrator for the UNIX servers, together hosting up to 150 web sites.
- Backed up the systems weekly to ensure that data was available for recovery purposes.
- Configured and managed Web server software, including MS Internet Information Server and Netscape Enterprise Server.
- Monitored and maintained Intranet and Internet web sites and provided weekly Web traffic and usage analysis reports using WebTrends Analysis Suite.
- Served as team lead on various server installation projects.
- Customized web site configuration to provide user-friendly development environments and convenient access for content management.

CUSTOMER SERVICE REPRESENTATIVE, TECHNICAL SERVICE TECHNICIAN (1992 – 1998)
Best Buy Stores, Inc., Colorado Springs, Colorado
- Successfully sold computer hardware and accessories, cellular telephones, digital satellite systems, software, and music in a retail setting.
- Won numerous sales awards for consistently meeting or exceeding revenue goals and selling value-added services.
- Handled returns and exchanges, placed service orders, and ensured customer satisfaction.
- Performed testing, troubleshooting, and minor repairs on consumer electronics.
- Managed shipping, receiving, and inventory of repair units.

ART EXHIBITIONS

STUDENT ART EXHIBITION (1996 – 1998)
Gallery of Contemporary Art, University of Colorado, Colorado Springs, Colorado
- Displayed a digital image and two sculptures.
- Won a Purchase Prize for a digital image entitled *Message from the Gods.* The image was purchased by the University for display in the University Center.

AARDVARK–ZYMURGY: THE WORKS OF UCCS ART GRADUATES (1997 – 1998)
The Warehouse Gallery, Colorado Springs, Colorado
- Displayed two sculptures and a digital image.

Chapter 11

At the bottom of your résumé (or sometimes toward the top), you can add anything else that might qualify you for your job objective. This includes licenses, certifications, special skills, publications, speeches, presentations, exhibits, grants, special projects, research, affiliations, and sometimes even interests if they truly relate. See the form at the end of this chapter to collect this information.

People often ask me what should NOT be included in a résumé. Well, there are very few times when photographs or personal information are appropriate on a résumé. Usually such facts only take up valuable white space, especially details such as age, sex, race, health, or marital status, and other information that potential employers are not allowed to ask anyway.

As I said before, however, there are exceptions to every rule in the résumé business! Here are some of them:

- Physicians who are following the American Medical Association approved format for a curriculum vita must include their place and date of birth and their citizenship.

- Submitting a résumé to a U.S. company doing business in certain foreign countries could be another example. On such a résumé, an Interests section would show a prospective employer that your hobbies are compatible with the host country.

- Students, or those who have recently graduated, often have a difficult time coming up with enough paid experience to demonstrate their qualifications. But, if they have held leadership positions in campus organizations or have supervised groups of people and organized activities on a volunteer basis, then an Activities section could strengthen those qualifications.

> Use your judgment. Only you know best what qualifications are important in your field.

- A list of sporting interests would be helpful for a person looking for a sports marketing position.

- International résumés in almost all cases require date of birth, place of birth, citizenship, marital status, sex, and often a photograph.

And the list goes on. It is important to use your judgment, since only you know best what qualifications are important in your field. For instance, several of my clients are ministers. In their line of work, it is very important to list a great deal of personal information that most employers would not need to know or even be allowed by law to request. In their case, the information they provide relates directly to bona fide occupational qualifications for the jobs they are seeking.

Photographs

Photographs on a résumé are required by foreign companies requesting a curriculum vita. However, in the United States, photographs are discouraged in all but a few industries. For instance, if you are trying for a job as an actor, model, newscaster, or in some other field where your appearance is, again, a bona fide occupational qualification, then a photograph is appropriate.

References

References are not usually presented on a résumé since most employers will not take the time to check references until after an interview. By then, they will have your completed application with a list of references. You also don't want to impose on your friends, associates, or former employers unnecessarily or too frequently. There is nothing wrong with taking a nicely printed list of personal references with you to an interview, however. The form at the end of this chapter will help you prepare that list.

Here's one of those exceptions to the rule again. If an advertisement requests that a list of references be sent with the résumé and cover letter, then by all means supply the list. You don't want to be accused of not following directions!

Another thing: Avoid that needless line at the bottom of the résumé that says, "References available upon request." It takes up valuable white space that you need to define the sections of your résumé in order to draw the reader's eyes logically down the page.

Pretend you are an interviewer. You ask, "Will you provide references?" The interviewee replies, "Sorry, no, I can't do that." Will you even think twice about continuing to consider this candidate? I think not. It is assumed that you will provide references when requested.

Samples

Here are some samples of additional information included in real résumés. Remember, each one had a bona fide reason for including this information. In other words, the information strengthened their qualifications in some way.

TECHNOLOGY SKILLS (when the goal is a network engineering job)

CERTIFICATIONS
- Microsoft Certified Professional (MCP).
- Certified in Microsoft Windows 2000 Pro.
- Certified in Microsoft Windows 2000 Server.
- Certified in Active Directory Administration and Design (March 2002).

NETWORKING
- Thorough understanding of all facets of networking, including the operation, design, and testing of voice, data, video, and imagery systems.
- Experienced in telecommunications network engineering, including RF, satellite communications, dedicated terrestrial, vines, packet switched networks, and encryption.
- Proficient in LAN and WAN provisioning, troubleshooting, operations, and administration.

HARDWARE
- **Mainframe Computer Systems and Architecture:** Tellabs DAX, Alcatel 600E, MUSIC, Streamliner, Newsdealer, TACINTEL, VAX 6000, DECstations, DEC PDP-11/70, GTE IS-1000.
- **Storage Devices:** magnetic tape drives, optical disk drives.
- **RF Equipment:** antennas, satellites, transmitters, receivers.
- **Digital Communications Equipment:** multiplexers, modems, key switching units, Voxtel PBX.
- **Imagery Systems:** FIST, DVITS, JDISS.
- **Cryptographic Devices:** STU-III, KG-84, KG-13, KG-6, KW-96.
- **Test Equipment:** Data Sentry 10, ADC Patch Panels, Firebird 6000, Logitech Test Generator, Halcyon Test Set, Sage 930 and 950, T-Com, T-Berd.

SOFTWARE
- **Operating Systems:** UNIX, Windows 2000/ME/NT 4.0/98/95/3.1, OS/2, MS-DOS.
- **Applications:** MS Word, Excel, Access, MS Project, Ami Pro, Quattro Pro, WordPerfect, Paradox, Lotus 1-2-3, Harvard Graphics.
- **Communication:** Netscape, Internet Explorer, cc:mail, ProComm, Net Term, PC Anywhere.
- **Other:** Help Desk Support Magic SQL, Remedy, SCO Open Server, PC Tools.

TECHNOLOGY SKILLS (for network/system administration)

Networking: Detailed understanding of networking concepts and architecture, including client/server and peer-to-peer networks. Experience with routers, switches, hubs, and coax/twisted pair cabling in Ethernet environments. Trained in TCP/IP, DUN, and IPX/SPX protocols. Experienced in Web development and server environments, including FrontPage, Microsoft IIS, VPNs, WWW browser applications, and client e-mail services.

Operating Systems: Windows 2000, Windows NT 4.0, Windows 95/98, MS-DOS, and UNIX.

Software: Remedy, MS Exchange, MS Word, Excel, PowerPoint, Access, MS Outlook/Web, Internet Explorer, SQL Server, Norton Antivirus Server/Client, Norton for Exchange, HP OpenView Network Node Manager, QIP for Windows (DNS), Sidewinder Firewall, and MS Proxy, among others.

Hardware: Detailed working knowledge and extensive experience with installing, troubleshooting, and performing maintenance on computers and support equipment, including network interface cards, sound cards, SCSI cards, tape drives, hard disks, JAZZ and ZIP drives, RAID, CD-ROMs, printers, plotters, etc. Experienced with Dell and Compaq servers, CISCO routers and switches, and Freevision KVM.

PRESENTATIONS (for nursing administration)

- *Pediatric Emergency Department Product Line Implementation,* Organization of Nurse Executives, New Jersey, March 2001.
- *Pediatric Education for Prehospital Professionals,* National Course Roll Out, Robert Wood Johnson University Hospital, New Brunswick, New Jersey, September 2000.
- *Financial Awareness of Hospital Nurses,* Robert Wood Johnson University Hospital, New Brunswick, New Jersey, May 2000.
- *Initiatives in Pediatric Emergency Services,* Board of Directors, Robert Wood Johnson University Hospital, New Brunswick, New Jersey, May 2000.
- *Hypothermia: Emergency Care of the Complex Patient,* Nursing Grand Rounds, CentraState Medical Center, Freehold, New Jersey, September 1998.
- *Newborn Care: Basic Assessment to Resuscitation,* Paramedic Curriculum, Robert Wood Johnson University Hospital, Emergency Medical Services Program, New Brunswick, New Jersey, June 1998, 1999, 2000, 2001.
- *Introduction to Pediatric Emergency Care,* Robert Wood Johnson University Hospital, New Brunswick, New Jersey, October 1998.
- Course Instructor for the Neonatal Resuscitation Program, Robert Wood Johnson University Hospital, New Brunswick, New Jersey, quarterly since January 1998.
- Course Instructor for Pediatric Advanced Life Support classes, Robert Wood Johnson University Hospital, New Brunswick, New Jersey, quarterly since January 1998.

AFFILIATIONS (for nursing administration)

- Executive Board Member, Seton Hall University Nursing Alumni (1999 – present)
- Member, American Nurses Association (ANA) (2002 – present)
- Member, New Jersey State Nurses Association (NJSNA) (2002 – present)
- Member, American Association of Nurse Executives (AONE) (2002 – present)
- Member, Gamma Nu Chapter, Nursing Honor Society (2001 – present)
- Member, Chair's Council of the College of Nursing (1997 – 1999)
- Peer Mentor, Sophomore and Junior Nursing Students (1997 – 1999)

- Member, Student Nurses Association, Seton Hall University (1995 – 1999)
  – President (1998 – 1999)
  – Delegate to the 1999 NSNA Convention, Pittsburgh, Pennsylvania
  – Delegate to the 1999 NJSNA Convention, Atlantic City, New Jersey
  – Publicity Chairperson (1997 – 1998)

AFFILIATIONS (for tourism management)

- Appointed to the Rules Committee of the Colorado Passenger Tramway Safety Board; created guidelines for funicular railway rules that were adopted nationwide (1983 – 1986).
- Member, Board of Directors, Pikes Peak Country Attractions Association (1991 – present); Executive Board Member (1996 – 1998), Vice President (1999 – 2000), and President (2000 – 2001).
- Member, Trees Committee, Pikes Peak Hospice (1987 – 1999); coordinated the installation of lighting on all trees for an annual fund-raising event that generates $135,000 a year.

CERTIFICATIONS (for nursing)

- Instructor, Pediatric Advanced Life Support (PALS)
- Instructor, Neonatal Resuscitation Program
- Instructor, Pediatric Emergency for Prehospital Providers
- Provider, Basic Life Support (BLS)
- Licensed Registered Nurse in Illinois and New Jersey

KEY CONTACTS (for public relations)

Print Media

- Newspapers: Sports editors, national sports columnists, and NBA columnists from the top 40 major newspapers and wire services, including *USA Today, The New York Times, Chicago Tribune, Los Angeles Times, The Wall Street Journal,* Associated Press, Bloomberg, Reuters, among others. Beat writers covering NBA teams in all 29 NBA markets, representing 100 major newspapers.
- Magazines: Top NBA and sports columnists from leading sports publications (*Sports Illustrated, The Sporting News, ESPN Magazine,* etc.) and mainstream news and business writers from *Time, Newsweek, Fortune, Business Week,* and others.

Television

- Network sports executives and on-air announcers and correspondents for major network and cable stations, including NBC, ESPN, HBO, TNT, Fox Sports, CNN, MSG Network, and others.
- A variety of contacts among on-air correspondents and producers from network television news departments, including NBC's *Meet the Press,* the *CBS Evening News,* and ABC's *20/20,* among others.

Sports

- Comprehensive working relationships with executives in the legal, marketing, and communications departments of professional sports leagues, unions, and teams.

- Broad contacts with a significant number of influential sports agents and many other player representatives concentrating in areas such as marketing, public relations, and financial planning.
- Extensive interaction with NBA players serving on the NBPA Executive and Negotiating Committees, and each NBA player serving as a team player representative over the past three years.

COMMUNITY SERVICE (for law enforcement)

- Member, Colorado Springs Workforce Management Council (1997 – present); Chairperson of the Recruitment Subcommittee for all city employees
- Board of Directors, National Alliance of the Mentally Ill (NAMI)
- Member, El Paso County Justice Advisory Council responsible for allocating resources for the jail population and addressing issues affecting law enforcement in the community
- Member, National Organization for Black Law Enforcement Executives (NOBLE)
- Member, International Association of Chiefs of Police (IACP)
- Member, 4th Judicial District Domestic Violence Recertification Board for health care providers (1996 – 1999)
- Member, School District 20 Principal Selection Committee (1995 – present)
- Served as liaison between the Police Department and the NAACP
- Worked with the Care Coalition Community Network to develop prevention programs for high-risk youth
- Member, Martin Luther King Jr. Holiday Committee
- Public Information Chairman for the Cinco de Mayo Committee
- Liaison to the Armed Forces Disciplinary Control Board
- Member, Consortium for the Developmentally Disabled
- Director and Past President of the Colorado Springs Police Athletic League
- Regional Chairman, National Police Athletic League

LEADERSHIP (for sports management)

U.S. Olympic Committee
- Member, Audit Committee (2001 – 2002)
- Appointed to the CEO Transition Team (2000 – 2001)
- Athletes Advisory Committee (1985 – 1992)

World Taekwondo Federation
- Vice Chair, Junior Committee (2001 – present)
- Member, Collegiate Committee (1998 – 2000)

U.S. Taekwondo Union
- Member, Executive Committee (1985 – 1998)
- Member, Coaching Science Committee (1985 – 1998)
- Member, National Tournament Committee (1985 – 1998)
- Member, Board of Directors (1984 – 1997)
- Chairman, Athletes Advisory Council (1985 – 1992)

Taekwondo Associations
- President, Big Sky Taekwondo Academy (1980 – 1991)
- President, Montana State Taekwondo Association (1984 – 1991)
- Chief Instructor, Montana State University (1980 – 1991)

Community Organizations
- Board of Directors, Citrus Heights Chamber of Commerce (1994 – 1997)
- Director of Workforce San Juan, a guidance program for at-risk youth (1994 – 1997)

VOLUNTEER EXPERIENCE (for admission to law school)

- Volunteered more than 130 hours to the Peterson Outdoor Adventure Program; served as a guide for all-terrain vehicle, water skiing, sailing, and canoe trips (1996 – 1998).
- Organized numerous community activities as a member of Beta Sigma Phi; donated baked goods monthly for the Center for Domestic Violence; raised more than $500 for the Circle of Hope Foundation; delivered holiday baskets for needy families (1995 – 1996).
- Fed homeless and needy families during the holidays; organized the entire military unit to assist for two years, feeding 500+ homeless at each event (1993 – 1996).
- Led neighbors in developing a local Neighborhood Watch program; collaborated with local Sheriff's deputies to provide signs and organize meetings to deter violence and crime (1995).
- Raised more than $500 in food, clothing, and toys for the needy at Christmas (1992 – 1995).
- Represented the military at the Colorado State Fair to provide the public with information about Cheyenne Mountain Air Force Base (1994).
- Organized a class at the Airman Leadership School to refurbish the Colorado Springs Ronald McDonald House (1994).
- Coordinated two very successful base-wide cookie drives to provide treats for military members stationed in the Middle East during the holiday season (1993 – 1994).
- Organized two holiday parties for residents of Laurel Manor Nursing Home (1992, 1994).
- Volunteered with Special Olympics; motivated participants during relay activities (1987).
- Raised hundreds of dollars for local charities by organizing the 21st Operation Group's annual "Slip-n-Slide" charity softball tournament (1993).

CERTIFICATIONS (for quality assurance)

Certified Quality Manager, American Society for Quality (2001 – present)
Certified RAB Quality System Auditor, RAB 16-hour Lead Auditor Course (1997)
Certified Quality Auditor, American Society for Quality (1996 – present)
Certificate of Quality Auditing, Pennsylvania State University (1996)
Certificate of Environmental Management System, Pennsylvania State University (1995)

LANGUAGES (for international jobs)

Spanish: Native tongue
English: Highly proficient, writing and speaking (PET, FIST Certificate, TOEFL, TSE, TWE)
Portuguese: Fluent speaking, proficient writing
French: Working knowledge (5 years Aliance Francaise)

PERSONAL DATA (for a physician following AMA format)

Born: Warner Robbins, Georgia, February 3, 1953
Citizenship: U.S.A.

CREDENTIALS FILE (for a recent graduate)

A credentials file is available from the University of Kansas upon request.

CREDENTIALS (for a teacher)

Colorado Professional Principal License (1998 – 2003)
Colorado Professional Administrator License (1998 – 2003)
- K–12 Director of Special Education Endorsement

Colorado Professional Teacher License (1998 – 2003)
- K–12 Aurally Handicapped Endorsement

LICENSES AND CERTIFICATIONS (for a nurse)

- Registered Nurse, State of Connecticut, E-34102
- Registered Nurse, State of Florida, RN-1932832
- Certified, Advanced Cardiac Life Support (ACLS)
- Certified, Basic Life Support (BLS)

RELATED QUALIFICATIONS

AFFILIATIONS (professional associations, chambers of commerce, Toastmasters, etc.) _____

_____

_____

_____

_____

_____

LANGUAGES (with levels of proficiency*) _____

_____

_____

*Fluent (absolute ability, native), Highly Proficient (3 to 5 years of usage in the country), Proficient (able to understand the subtleties of the language), Working Knowledge (can conduct everyday business), Knowledge (exposure to the language, courtesy phrases)

LICENSES _____

_____

_____

_____

CERTIFICATIONS _____

_____

_____

_____

CREDENTIALS _____

_____

_____

_____

PRESENTATIONS/SPEECHES (title, meeting, sponsoring organization, city, state, date) _____

_____

_____

_____

EXHIBITS _____

_____

_____

_____

PUBLICATIONS (authors, article title, publication title, volume, issue, page numbers, date) _____

_____

_____

_____

GRANTS _____

_____

_____

_____

RELATED QUALIFICATIONS

SPECIAL PROJECTS _____
_____
_____
_____

RESEARCH _____
_____
_____
_____

UNIQUE SKILLS _____
_____
_____
_____

VOLUNTEER ACTIVITIES, CIVIC CONTRIBUTIONS _____
_____
_____
_____
_____
_____
_____

HONORS, AWARD, DISTINCTIONS, PROFESSIONAL RECOGNITION _____
_____
_____
_____

COMPUTERS _____
_____

Applications (MS Word, Excel, PowerPoint, etc.) _____
Operating Systems (Windows, Macintosh, UNIX, etc.) _____
Databases (Access, Oracle, etc.) _____
Programming Languages _____
Networking _____
Communications _____
Hardware _____

OTHER RELEVANT SKILLS _____
_____

Actors (singing, musical instruments, martial arts, etc.) _____
Secretaries (typing speed, shorthand, etc.) _____
Welders (TIG, MIG, ARC, etc.) _____

INTERNATIONAL (travel, living, cross-cultural skills, etc.) _____
_____
_____
_____

OTHER RELATED QUALIFICATIONS

_____
_____
_____
_____
_____
_____
_____
_____
_____
_____
_____
_____
_____
_____
_____
_____
_____
_____
_____
_____
_____
_____
_____
_____
_____
_____

REFERENCES

Unless an advertisement specifically requests references, don't send them with your résumé. Type a nice list of three to six references on the same letterhead as your résumé to take with you to the interview. Use this form to collect the information for your reference list. Choose people who know how you work and are not just personal friends or family members.

NAME _____
RELATIONSHIP TO YOU _____
COMPANY _____
MAILING ADDRESS _____
CITY, STATE, ZIP _____
WORK PHONE _____ CELL PHONE _____
HOME PHONE _____ E-MAIL _____

NAME _____
RELATIONSHIP TO YOU _____
COMPANY _____
MAILING ADDRESS _____
CITY, STATE, ZIP _____
WORK PHONE _____ CELL PHONE _____
HOME PHONE _____ E-MAIL _____

NAME _____
RELATIONSHIP TO YOU _____
COMPANY _____
MAILING ADDRESS _____
CITY, STATE, ZIP _____
WORK PHONE _____ CELL PHONE _____
HOME PHONE _____ E-MAIL _____

NAME _____
RELATIONSHIP TO YOU _____
COMPANY _____
MAILING ADDRESS _____
CITY, STATE, ZIP _____
WORK PHONE _____ CELL PHONE _____
HOME PHONE _____ E-MAIL _____

NAME _____
RELATIONSHIP TO YOU _____
COMPANY _____
MAILING ADDRESS _____
CITY, STATE, ZIP _____
WORK PHONE _____ CELL PHONE _____
HOME PHONE _____ E-MAIL _____

NAME _____
RELATIONSHIP TO YOU _____
COMPANY _____
MAILING ADDRESS _____
CITY, STATE, ZIP _____
WORK PHONE _____ CELL PHONE _____
HOME PHONE _____ E-MAIL _____

Step 11 Qualifications Summary

We really are almost done! One last thing before you put it all together. Think about the objective (or focus) that you determined in Step 1 of Chapter 2. Rewrite this objective on the form at the end of this chapter, then write four or five sentences that give an overview of your qualifications.

This profile, or qualifications summary, should be placed at the beginning of your résumé. You can include some of your personal traits or special skills that might have been difficult to get across in your job descriptions. Some HR professionals might disagree with me. They say that they skip over descriptions of unverifiable claims about personal strengths, but there are just as many HR managers who read every word. Besides, you want to make sure you cover your soft skills for electronic résumés where keywords defined in job requisitions often request such strengths.

Here is a sample profile section for a computer systems technician looking for a job with a military contractor:

- Experienced systems/network technician with significant communications and technical control experience in the military sector.
- Focused and hard working; willing to go the extra mile for the customer.
- Skilled in troubleshooting complex problems by thinking outside the box.
- Possesses a high degree of professionalism and dedication to exceptional quality.
- Current Top Secret security clearance with access to Sensitive Compartmentalized Information.

It is also acceptable to use a keyword summary like the one below to give a "quick and dirty" look at your qualifications:

- **Hardware:** IBM 360/370, S/390, 303X, 308X, ES-9000, Amdahl V6-II, V7, V8, 3705/ 3725, Honeywell 6000, PDP II, NOVA, Eclipse, Interdata 8/32, Wang OIS 115, 140, VS-80, VS-100, HP 3000, 9000, Vectra, IBM PC-AT, XT, and numerous other computers and mainframes.

> *Recruiters spend as little as ten seconds deciding whether to read a résumé from top to bottom.*

- **Languages:** FORTRAN, PL/1, COBOL, BASIC, BAL (ALC), JCL, APL, DL/1, SQL, DS-2, HP-UX, and various PC-oriented software and support packages.
- **Systems:** DOS, OS, CICS, VSI/II, MVS, SVS, VM/CMS, IMS, MVT-II, MFT, POWER, TOTAL, DATANET-30, JES-2, JES-3, BTAM, QTAM, TCAM, VTAM, TSO, ACF, NCP, SNA, SAA, ESCON, SDLC, X-25, TCP/IP, UNIX, and TELNET.

This type of laundry list isn't very interesting for a human being to read, but a few recruiters in high-tech industries like this list of terms because it gives them a quick overview of an applicant's skills. You can use whichever style you prefer.

Busy recruiters spend as little as ten seconds deciding whether to read a résumé from top to bottom. You will be lucky if the first third of your résumé gets read, so make sure the information at the top entices the reader to read it all.

This profile section must be relevant to the type of job for which you are applying. It might be true that you are "compassionate," but will it help you get a job as a high-pressure salesperson? Write this profile from the perspective of a potential employer. What will convince this person to call you instead of someone else?

Samples

Let's look at some sample profiles for various industries. You will notice some significantly different styles of presenting the information. Choose the style that best presents your information.

ACCOUNTANT

- Dedicated accountant with thirteen years of diverse experience that includes:
  - Public accounting
  - Nonprofit accounting
  - Tax preparation
  - Internal auditing
  - Compliance auditing
  - Reporting
- Certified Public Accountant in California and Colorado; Certified Internal Auditor.
- Analytical and thorough professional with a track record of success managing the toughest assignments.
- Effective team player with exceptional communication, writing, and interpersonal skills.

ARTIST

- Creative graphic artist with experience in pen and ink illustration, watercolor, and oil mediums.
- Background in magazine/book, children's book, graphic novel, and comic book illustration.
- Hard-working, loyal artist with definitive leadership and sales abilities.
- Self-starter; able to motivate others to perform to their maximum potential.

ATTORNEY

- Licensed attorney in private practice since 1969 (Colorado and New Mexico).
- Board Certified Civil Trial Specialist, National Board of Trial Advocacy, with extensive litigation experience (initially certified 1980, recertified 1985, 1990, and 1995).
- Recognized specialist in workers' compensation law by the New Mexico Legal Specialization Board.
- Admitted to practice before the U.S. Court of Appeals, 10th Circuit; U.S. District Court for the District of New Mexico; U.S. District Court for the Western District of Texas; District Courts of the State Colorado; and all courts in the State of New Mexico.
- Successful Federal Administrative Law Judge applicant (awaiting placement).
- Extensive experience in the preparation and trial of injury claims resulting from both workers' compensation and off-the-job injuries.
- Exceptional knowledge of administrative procedures, rules of evidence, and trial practices.
- Able to communicate in a clear, concise manner with people of diverse backgrounds and levels of authority.

BOOKKEEPER

- Experienced bookkeeper and administrator with twenty years of diverse experience.
- Background in management, general ledger, financial statements, accounts payable, accounts receivable, and payroll.
- Computer literate in Windows, QuickBooks Pro, One-Write, MS Word, Excel, and Business Works.
- Dependable, accurate, and well organized; able to handle multiple tasks simultaneously.

BUYER

- Dependable, efficient procurement professional with 13 years of experience in the grocery business.
- Quick learner who is able to troubleshoot complex problems and multitask effectively.
- Self-motivated team player with exceptional communication and interpersonal skills.
- Proven leader who enjoys finding better ways of doing things and making value-added improvements.

CERTIFIED PUBLIC ACCOUNTANT, FINANCIAL EXECUTIVE

- Experienced Financial Executive and Certified Public Accountant with a strong background in:
  - Accounting
  - Budgeting
  - Credit Management
  - Reporting
  - MIS
  - Administration
  - HR Management
  - Benefits
  - Acquisitions
  - Banking Relationships
  - Environmental Compliance
  - Legal Issues
- CFO at the time of an initial public offering; supervised SEC reporting and investor relations.
- Managed preparation of the first registered Internet public venture capital offering and several private placements to accredited investors.
- Negotiated a variety of long-term and short-term loan syndications and developed cash management functions.
- Licensed CPA in Arizona and Ohio (inactive); won the Silver Award for the second highest exam grade in Ohio.

CHILD CARE PROVIDER

- Dedicated child care provider with more than eleven years of experience.
- Fair and just with a commitment to setting a good example.
- Patient instructor who enjoys working with children.
- Effective team player with strong interpersonal and communication skills.

CONSTRUCTION PROFESSIONAL

- Experienced construction professional with a background in residential and commercial roofing and general contracting.
- Quality oriented with a dedication to getting the job done right the first time.
- Well-organized with a natural aptitude for math; skilled in analyzing tasks and breaking them down into manageable pieces.

CONSULTANT

- Detail-oriented consultant with a strong entrepreneurial spirit and a background in consultative selling and MIS.
- Experience with e-business, competitive strategy development, strategic business planning, re-engineering, custom development, data-driven models, process assessment/improvement, and information technology.
- Extensive background in international marketing, importing, advertising design, and new business development.
- Proven history of building new business by identifying, calling on, and driving business decisions at the executive level.
- High-energy team player with exceptional leadership, analytical, problem solving, communication, and presentation skills.

CRIMINAL INVESTIGATOR

- Experienced criminal investigator with 18 years as a Deputy U.S. Marshal with full law enforcement authority and a background in management, investigative, and supervisory positions.
- Dedicated manager who welcomes a challenge.
- Team player who is willing to work long hours to get the job done.
- Proven reputation for working well with others and serving as a role model/mentor.

EDITOR, BOOK PUBLISHING

- Experienced editor with a strong book publishing background, including:

– Math	– Medical	– Business	– Juvenile
– Science	– Nursing	– Art	– Parenting
– Test Preparation	– Allied Health	– Gardening	– Child Care

- Skilled wordsmith with the ability to transform a rough draft into a marketable finished product.
- Effective team player with outstanding communication and interpersonal skills.
- Knowledge of Windows, MS Word, Excel, WordPerfect, Internet browsers, and e-mail.

EMT/FIREFIGHTER

- Experienced EMT and registered firefighter with a strong desire to help people.
- Quick thinker who enjoys a fast pace and the challenge of a job's physical demands.
- Adept at working under pressure and managing multiple tasks simultaneously.
- Effective team player with a positive attitude and strong interpersonal skills.
- Proven problem solver who enjoys getting to the root of a challenge.

ELECTRONICS TECHNICIAN

- Experienced electronics technician with a strong background in test and engineering.
- Detail-oriented and analytical; able to manage the details while seeing the whole picture.
- Respected for the ability to solve problems and get things done when others give up.
- Effective team player with exceptional communication and interpersonal skills.

ENGINEER

- Experienced engineering professional with a strong background in:
  - Quality control/quality assurance
  - Electrical/mechanical systems
  - Precision-process maintenance
  - Analysis and problem solving
  - Equipment fabrication
  - Test equipment operation
  - Electronic principles and theories
  - Computer-controlled devices
- Proven expertise in engineering enhancements to fabrication tools, chemical mechanical polishing, vacuum systems, pneumatic systems, diffusion, and gas delivery systems.
- Skilled in reading and interpreting blueprints, engineering prints, and other schematic drawings.

EXECUTIVE SECRETARY

- Experienced executive secretary with a strong work ethic and proven customer service skills.
- Quick learner who enjoys the challenge of new responsibilities.
- Effective team player who is dependable, cooperative, and able to work under tight deadlines.
- Strong communication and interpersonal skills; tactful when working with difficult people.

FACILITY MAINTENANCE

- Experienced technician with a diverse background in industrial and commercial facility maintenance.
- Nationally Certified Apartment Maintenance Technician (CAMT) since 2000.
- HVAC Certified (Universal), Esco Institute since 1993; EPA Certified since 1996.
- Dependable, loyal worker who can fix just about anything and learns quickly.
- Personable and courteous; proven track record of exceptional customer service.
- Good listener with a quick sense of humor and the ability to work well with all types of people.
- Exceptional attendance record; never missed a page call in eight years of 24-hour-a-day availability.

FIELD ENGINEER, TELECOM

- Experienced field engineer, cable splicer, communications technician, and supervisor.
- Background in the installation, testing, and maintenance of analog/digital telephone and central office equipment.
- Self-motivated team player who works well independently and manages time efficiently.
- Long track record of perfect attendance with no on-the-job accidents.
- Flexible worker with the ability to analyze and prioritize project assignments.
- Proven reputation for providing exceptional customer service.

FINANCIAL PLANNER

- Experienced financial planner with proven expertise in retirement planning, investments, insurance, and asset management.
- Hold current Series 7, 63, 65, 31, life, health, and accident insurance licenses.
- Committed to the highest levels of integrity and professional ethics.
- Team leader with exceptional communication skills and an engaging interpersonal style.
- Able to work effectively with people from diverse backgrounds and levels of authority.
- Knowledge of Windows, MS Word, WordPerfect, Outlook, e-mail, and the Internet.

FINANCE PROFESSIONAL

- Seasoned finance professional with extensive experience in:
  - Venture capital
  - Mergers/acquisitions
  - Business plan analysis
  - Business valuation
  - Due diligence
  - Financial modeling
  - Operations management
  - Strategic planning
  - New business development
- Multi-disciplinary executive with a diverse background in marketing/sales, finance, accounting loan origination and servicing, and public accounting.
- Able to effectively motivate both management and operating personnel to achieve maximum results.
- Skilled in applying logical but creative approaches to problem resolution.

HIGH TECH or CORPORATE TRAINING

- Eight years of experience as an **Instruction Designer** and **Trainer** in both the corporate and public sectors.
- Strong background in developing company training programs, computer-based instruction, and corporate university programs.
- Skilled in organization, leadership, project management, team building, and problem solving.
- Effective team player with proven interpersonal, communication, presentation, and writing skills.

INFORMATION ANALYST

- Dedicated information analyst with more than 18 years of programming/data processing experience in the telecommunications, banking, and government sectors.
- Certified Xenix Systems Administrator.

- Skilled in analysis, construction, implementation, troubleshooting, production support, operations support, help desk, testing (unit, regression, integration, and systems), training, and maintenance.
- Detail oriented and organized; comfortable taking the initiative and working independently.

LAW ENFORCEMENT

- Proven leader with more than twenty years of law enforcement experience and expertise in program development, project management, team motivation, and public relations.
- Service-oriented professional with the ability to promote positive organizational values.
- Personally dedicated to ensuring the delivery of quality service.
- Experienced public speaker with strong communication and presentation skills.

LOGISTICIAN, MATERIALS MANAGER

HIGHLIGHTS OF QUALIFICATIONS

Experienced materials manager and gifted logistician with a proven background in:
Administration • Operations • Contract Negotiations • Cost Control • Budgeting
Forecasting • Purchasing • Automated Inventory Tracking Systems • Transportation • Distribution
Self-motivated leader with strong interpersonal, communication, and motivation skills.
Able to organize and prioritize multiple projects with divergent needs.
Hold a current Secret security clearance.

MANAGER, GENERAL

- Forward-thinking manager with diverse experience in:
  - Business development
  - Change management
  - Process re-engineering
  - Strategic planning
  - Consultative selling
  - Marketing
  - Employee development
  - Training and facilitation
  - Supervision
- Skilled in applying logical but creative approaches to problem resolution.
- Self-motivated; comfortable working independently and taking the initiative.
- Effective team player with exceptional communication and presentation skills.

MANAGER, GENERAL

- Experienced manager with a proven track record of improving productivity and profitability.
- Resourceful at finding innovative solutions to complex problems.
- Able to work outside the job description and to manage crises with ease.
- Personable team player with strong communication and interpersonal skills.

MANAGER, HEALTHCARE

- Self-motivated healthcare manager with a passion for taking on new responsibilities.
- Proven supervisor with the ability to motivate workers and lead by example.
- Skilled in applying logical but creative approaches to problem resolution.
- Open to re-evaluating traditional methods and finding better ways to get the job done.
- Personable team player with strong communication and presentation skills.

MANAGER, HUMAN RESOURCES

Well-rounded human resource management professional offering
more than five years of experience in:
Recruiting • Interviewing • Employee Selection • Placement • Job Descriptions
Position Evaluation • Training • Discipline • Workers' Compensation • Pay
EEOC Compliance • Labor Relations • ADA • FMLA

MANAGER, TOURISM/HOSPITALITY

- Adaptable manager with nine years of experience in the tourism/hospitality industry, including:
  - Strategic planning
  - Multi-property management
  - Budgeting and operations
  - Marketing and promotion
  - Personnel development
  - Public/guest relations
  - Reservation sales
  - Revenue maximization
  - New property construction
- Confident leader who is able to motivate employees to excel in customer service.
- Effective team player with excellent communication and interpersonal skills.
- Self-motivated professional with a strong work ethic and proven problem-solving skills.

MANUFACTURING

- Sixteen years of manufacturing experience from research and development phase to high-volume production requirements.
- Skilled in the development of documentation and procedures to meet regulatory requirements.
- Able to work equally well on an independent basis or as a cooperative team member.
- Excellent leadership and organizational skills; strong oral and written communication abilities.

MEDICAL ASSISTANT

- Registered Medical Assistant with an Associate Degree in medical assisting.
- Experienced in recordkeeping, filing, typing (55 wpm), scheduling, phone etiquette, dictation, and most office machines.
- Knowledge of computers; experienced with WordPerfect and MEDISOFT; familiar with many other Windows and MS-DOS applications.
- Responsible and dependable professional with a strong medical ethic.
- Excellent organizer who is able to work independently and as part of a team.

MENTAL HEALTH PROFESSIONAL

- Experienced mental health professional with a diverse background in inpatient and medical psychiatric assessment and therapy, including:
  - Social work
  - Individual therapy
  - Group therapy
  - Evaluation
  - Disposition
  - Domestic violence
  - Crisis intervention
  - Suicide prevention
  - Chemical dependency
- Certified Alcohol Counselor I (CACI) in the state of Colorado.
- Innovative, highly energetic worker with demonstrated organizational and social skills.
- Able to accept and appreciate differences in others; nonjudgmental and impartial.
- Sensitive and empathetic team player with finely tuned communication and interpersonal abilities.

NURSE

- Dedicated Interventional Cardiology Nurse with a reputation for astute clinical judgment.
- Respected professional with a strong background in critical care nursing and pharmacology.
- Compassionate caregiver who quickly establishes and maintains rapport with patients.
- Detail-oriented and precise; dedicated to providing excellence in patient care.
- Adept at managing multiple tasks simultaneously and working under pressure.
- Knowledge of Windows, computerized charting, and electronic cardiac systems.

NURSE ADMINISTRATOR

- Dedicated nurse administrator who enjoys new challenges and works well in high-pressure environments demanding hard work and self-motivation.
- Licensed Registered Nurse (New Jersey 120960) with graduate education in health systems administration and business management.
- Effective team leader with proven communication, interpersonal, and presentation skills.
- Detail-oriented professional with strong problem-solving abilities.
- Compassionate caregiver who is able to quickly establish and maintain rapport with patients and other healthcare providers.

NURSING

- Registered Nurse, Washington, RN 00100096
- Registered Nurse, California, RN 289035
- Certified Emergency Nurse, 9606587
- National Registry Paramedic, PO 856139
- Certified Emergency Medical Technician, Washington
- PADI Dive Master and Rescue Diver, 23415
- Advanced Cardiac Life Support (ACLS)
- Pediatric Advanced Life Support (PALS)
- Certified PALS Instructor
- Prehospital Trauma Life Support (PHTLS)

OCCUPATIONAL THERAPIST

- Compassionate occupational therapist with an enthusiasm for helping others.
- Persuasive motivator with an inherent understanding of people and a genuine caring attitude.
- Effective team player who works well with others and strives to create win-win relationships.
- Able to collaborate with other healthcare professionals to develop productive treatment plans.

OFFICE WORKER

- Dependable office worker with more than five years of hands-on experience.
- Able to thrive in a fast-paced environment, managing multiple tasks simultaneously.
- Versatile, quick learner who loves challenge and adapts well to new situations.
- Self-motivated; work well with little or no supervision.
- Knowledge of Windows, MS Word, Excel, Access, and SQL computer software.
- Skills: typing, ten-key, fax, copiers, laser printers, and multiple phone lines.

PILOT

- Experienced leader with a proven track record in aviation operations and safety management.
- Diverse background as a pilot with strong technical and training skills.
- Current FAA Commercial Pilot License with rotorcraft and instrument ratings.
- Ambitious professional who adapts quickly to changing conditions.

PROJECT MANAGER

- Experienced project manager with a proven background in the development and implementation of complex computer and communication networks.
- Dedicated professional who is skilled at identifying process improvements and developing quality solutions that are faster, cheaper, and better.
- Effective team leader with strong communication and interpersonal skills.
- Current top secret security clearance with special background investigation (TS/SBI), SCI reinstatable.

PUBLIC RELATIONS

- Seasoned public relations expert with a vast range of industry and media contacts.
- Nationally recognized spokesman, commentator, and expert on the business and law of sports.
- Strong background in sports journalism with major newspapers, radio stations, and television networks.
- Quick thinker who is skilled at applying logical but creative approaches to challenges.

PUBLIC RELATIONS

- Creative and versatile public relations professional with a strong desire to succeed.
- Self-motivated, articulate team player with exceptional speaking and writing skills.
- Proficient researcher with proven experience using MediaMap, Lexis-Nexis, databases, the Internet, search engines, Windows, and PowerPoint.
- Quick learner who is committed to keeping abreast of advancements in his field and who derives satisfaction from a hard day's work.

SALES AND MARKETING POSITION

- Demonstrated success in sales and management positions for more than 17 years.
- Proven ability to develop new markets and maintain profitable client relationships.
- Consistent high achiever recognized for exceptional sales accomplishments with fiercely competitive products in a shrinking marketplace.
- Respected for powerful negotiating and closing abilities.
- Self-motivated and focused; comfortable working independently with little supervision.

SENIOR EXECUTIVE

- High-energy senior executive with a demonstrated track record of success in:
  - Sales/marketing
  - Finance
  - Strategic planning
  - Technical innovations
  - Business development
  - Negotiations
  - Operations management
  - International business
  - Staff development
- Proven ability to combine high-caliber analytical and strategic planning skills with outstanding business development and marketing expertise in both domestic and global business arenas.
- Fast-track professional who thrives on challenges and takes a hands-on leadership role to position the company for growth in a changing environment.
- Recognized for ingenuity, integrity, and the ability to negotiate win/win scenarios.

SOCIAL WORKER

- Empathetic medical social worker with experience in:
  - Special needs children
  - Counseling/advocacy
  - Part C funding
  - Case management
  - Training
  - Service coordination
  - Abuse and neglect
  - Team building
  - Facilitation
- Self-motivated with a commitment to providing quality care.
- Creative professional who enjoys a challenge and sees the big picture.
- Excellent knowledge of IFSP and IEP processes, best practices in early intervention, legal rights of the special education population, and the health problems and medical needs of children.
- Extensive network of community resources on the Front Range in education, mental health, pediatric services, healthcare, and human services.

SUPERINTENDENT, GOLF COURSE

- Experienced golf course superintendent focused on efficient operations, exceptional attention to detail, and the highest level of course conditioning and playability for the perfect golf experience.
- Ten years of experience in greenskeeping and golf course management.
- Skilled administrator who leads by example and promotes a strong team work ethic.
- Extensive knowledge of horticulture, including an undergraduate degree in landscape horticulture/turf management.

TEACHER

- Dedicated teacher with the desire to instill in children the passion to be life-long learners.
- Able to set and maintain high expectations with the belief that children will rise to them and be reliable, respectful, responsible, and ready to learn.
- Outgoing and patient instructor who enjoys working with children.
- Effective team player with strong communication and interpersonal skills.

TECHNICIAN, TELECOMMUNICATIONS

- Self-motivated telecommunications technician with 14 years of diverse experience.
- Expertise in the installation, troubleshooting, and repair of digital and analog communications, teleconferencing, video, and computer network equipment.
- Respected for the ability to solve complex problems and to get things done when others give up.
- Thrives in fast-paced, challenging environments; holds a current secret security clearance.

TRAINER, INSTRUCTIONAL DESIGNER

- Experienced trainer, instructional designer, manager, and change agent with a background in both corporate and academic environments.
- **Training:** Creative presenter, facilitator, and coach with strong communication and interpersonal skills. Proven ability to use innovative delivery methods and group dynamics to improve the quality of the training experience. Adept at teaching across a wide variety of cultural differences.
- **Problem Solving:** Conceptual thinker who enjoys the challenge of analyzing systems and making them more effective. Experienced organizational developer who has conducted focus groups and sensing interviews to design departmental improvements.
- **Teamwork:** Collaborative team player with the ability to motivate others and build strong teams that can work together to accomplish an organization's goals.
- **Certifications:** Ropes Course Trainer. Mager Criterion Referenced Instructor. Train the Trainer. Myers-Briggs Type Indicator, FIRO-B, Strong, and Campbell instruments.

CONTACT INFORMATION

This final stage of information gathering will provide you with all the information you need to begin your résumé. For the contact information, you can use your full name, first and last name only, or shortened names (Pat Criscito instead of Patricia K. Criscito).

Do not use work telephone numbers or a work e-mail address on your résumé. Potential employers tend to consider that an abuse of company resources, which implies you might do the same if you are working for them. Listing a cellular telephone number on your résumé gives a hiring manager a way to reach you during working hours.

Avoid the use of "cutesy" e-mail addresses on a résumé. If you use *babycakes@aol.com* for your personal e-mail, create a second e-mail address under your account that will be more professional. If your only access to the Internet is at work, then create a free-mail account at *hotmail.com, juno.com, usa.net, yahoo.com, mail.com, excite.com, e-mail.com,* or *altavista.com.* Check *www.refdesk.com/freemail.html* for a list of even more free e-mail services.

NAME _____

ADDRESS _____

CITY/STATE/ZIP _____

COUNTRY (if applying outside the country where you live)_____

HOME PHONE _____   CELL PHONE _____

E-MAIL _____

WEB SITE _____

QUALIFICATIONS PROFILE

Keep the qualifications profile short, sweet, and to the point. I tend to limit them to five or six bullets, although there are exceptions to this rule when creating a curriculum vita or other types of professional résumés. I'll give you a few extra places to list that information if you need a longer profile, but try to use no more than six of the blanks.

You can title this section with any of the following headlines: Profile, Qualifications, Highlights of Qualifications, Expertise, Strengths, Summary, Synopsis, Background, Professional Background, Executive Summary, Highlights, Overview, Professional Overview, Capsule, or Keyword Profile.

OBJECTIVE/FOCUS (this can become the first sentence of your profile or stand alone) _____
_____
_____
_____

SECOND SENTENCE (areas of expertise) _____
_____
_____
_____

STRENGTHS _____
_____
_____
_____

STRENGTHS _____
_____
_____
_____

STRENGTHS _____
_____
_____
_____

STRENGTHS _____
_____
_____
_____

STRENGTHS _____
_____
_____
_____

STRENGTHS _____
_____
_____
_____

Chapter 13

Now it's time to put this all together into the perfect résumé. You have a qualifications summary, your education, experience, and other relevant information. How do you decide which section goes first, second, third, and last? That depends . . . everything in the résumé business depends!

Start with the section that contains your strongest qualifications for your target job. If you have had little experience in your prospective field but have a degree that qualifies you for a starting position in the industry, then by all means list your education first. Most people eventually move their education below their experience as they get further from their school days. If you change your career and go back to school, then the education will move to the top again and begin to gravitate to the bottom as you gain relevant experience.

The same idea goes for information within each section. For instance, if your job title is more impressive than where you worked, then list it first.

VICE PRESIDENT OF MARKETING
Little Known Company, Boulder, Colorado

IBM CORPORATION, Boulder, Colorado
Assistant Export Coordinator

Functional or Chronological

There are three basic types of résumés—reverse chronological, functional, and a combination of the two. There are fad styles that come and go, but the three I've just mentioned are the classics.

A reverse-chronological résumé arranges your experience and education in chronological order with the most recent dates first. This style is the most popular résumé with recruiters and hiring managers. It showcases your jobs one at a time and shows a clear chronology of your work history. Use it:

Everything in the résumé business depends.

1. When your last job is a strong foundation for your current objective.

2. When you are staying in the same field as your past job(s).

3. When you have a strong history of promotion or development in your career.

4. When your prior titles or company names are an asset to your current job search.

5. When you are in a highly traditional field (education, banking, government, etc.).

6. When you are working with an executive recruiter.

Most of the résumés I write are reverse-chronological, but that doesn't mean a different type of résumé might not fit your needs better. A functional résumé organizes your work experience by the functions you performed regardless of date. The functional résumé highlights your skills and potential instead of your work history. Use it:

1. When you want to play down gaps in your experience.

2. When you are entering the job market for the first time.

3. When you are reentering the job market, for example after raising children.

4. When you want to change careers.

5. When you have changed jobs too many times or have lots of jobs to show because you have been doing consulting, freelance, or temporary work.

6. When you have done the same things in every job and don't want to use the same descriptions over and over again.

7. When you need to de-emphasize your age but exploit older experience.

8. When you need to list volunteer experience and community or school activities to strengthen your qualifications.

List your functional paragraphs in their order of importance, with the items listed first that will help you get the particular job you are targeting. Refer to Step 9 in Chapter 10 of this book for ideas on how to rearrange your résumé sentences to better capture your reader's attention.

You should know that there are very rare times when I would recommend a purely functional résumé, however. In the 1980s, true functional résumés developed a bad reputation because applicants were not listing where they gained their experience. It made recruiters suspicious that the applicant was trying to hide something. A combination functional/chronological résumé will avoid this problem. Always list a brief synopsis of your actual work experience at the bottom of your functional résumé with each title, employer, and the dates worked.

Here are some sample functional/chronological combination résumés that might help you decide if this style is right for you.

Leesa A. Murphy

ADDRESS — 12345 Anywhere Street, Newtown, Colorado 80907 (719) 555-1234

PROFILE

- Dedicated administrative assistant with 7+ years experience in the judicial court system.
- Self-starter with strong problem solving and organizational abilities.
- Demonstrated ability to handle difficult situations with tact.
- Skilled in analyzing a task and breaking it down into manageable pieces.
- Team player with exceptional communication and interpersonal skills.
- Knowledge of WordPerfect, Windows, Excel, and proprietary systems.

EXPERIENCE

LEGAL EXPERIENCE

- Coordinated and set court dockets and dates, prepared juries for trial, and assisted pro se individuals.
- Created new files, maintained filing system, and typed judge's directives, orders, and letters.
- Collected traffic fines, managed collections registry for criminal/juvenile cases, and assisted in the collections process by turning cases over to State Collections.
- Worked closely with the Department of Labor in the investigation of employment status and wage garnishments; met with 20 to 30 people per day.
- Maintained the personnel expense reimbursement program (COFORS).
- Set appointments for 30 probation officers.
- Performed intake and input new cases in the computer system.
- Routed mail and copied files for the District Attorney's office.
- Entered data for child support and domestic cases.

ADMINISTRATION/MANAGEMENT

- Developed and implemented all office procedures for the recovery center.
- Accountable for the establishment and preparation of financial statements, insurance billings, monthly and daily accounting reports.
- Reviewed all deposits, accounts receivable, and insurance payments.
- Analyzed, negotiated, and resolved problem accounts.
- Supervised and evaluated office personnel.
- Issued demand letters, negotiated repayments/settlements, developed payment plans, and processed collection paperwork.
- Improved monthly accounts receivable status ratings from below standard (a $40,000 deficit) to 98% in less than a year.
- Developed systems for work flow and record keeping that significantly improved efficiency.

OTHER EXPERIENCE

- Extensive public relations and customer service background.
- Excel in dealing with difficult people and situations.
- Provided secretarial support and front desk reception services.
- Processed military personnel paperwork for transitions, issued passports, and maintained records.

WORK HISTORY

Municipal Court Clerk, Municipal Court, Colorado Springs, Colorado	1999 – present
Collections Investigator, 4th Judicial District Court, Colorado Springs, Colorado	1998 – 1999
Assistant Division Clerk, 4th Judicial District Court, Colorado Springs, Colorado	1997 – 1998
Court Clerk II, 4th Judicial District Court, Colorado Springs, Colorado	1994 – 1997
Secretary I, 4th Judicial District Court, Colorado Springs, Colorado	1993 – 1994
Office Manager, Lakeside Recovery Center, Tacoma, Washington	1991 – 1992
Administrative Assistant, United States Army	1983 – 1991

EDUCATION

Pikes Peak Community College, 3 hour course in Psychology
Kansas State University, 12 hours of liberal arts studies
Central Texas College, 6 hours of liberal arts studies

ADDRESS

12345 Anywhere Street, Newtown, Colorado 80907   (719) 555-1234

119

MICHAEL D. NEWMAN

Phone: (781) 555-1245   20 Anywhere Street ▪ Newtown, Massachusetts 02368   mnewman@protypeltd.com

PROFILE

- Experienced Advertising Director with demonstrated success in:
  - Major accounts
  - Classified advertising
  - Retail accounts
  - Research
  - New product development
  - Sales and training
  - Budgeting
  - Graphic arts and production
  - Planning and scheduling
- Practical problem solver with exceptional analytical, creative, and communication skills.
- Strong background in building new territories and using creative marketing approaches.
- Demonstrated ability to create client loyalty above and beyond the sales relationship.
- Proficient in Windows 95, MS Word, Excel, PowerPoint, Access, Quark, AIM billing system, and ATEX classified front-end software.

EXPERIENCE

Major Accounts

- Managed the major accounts sales team for *The Gazette,* a Freedom Corporation newspaper with a circulation of 121,000.
- Made sales presentations to senior management of major accounts in cities nationwide.
- Developed a new client base and expanded existing accounts to achieve $17 million in annual sales.

Research and New Product Development

- Directed the development of new products for *The Gazette,* including demographic and psychographic market research, feasibility studies, product design and packaging, budgeting, scheduling, implementation, sales, and P&L.
- Analyzed statistical and other market data and used the results to create sales presentations to advertisers; researched and analyzed competitive information.
- Developed the *Home in Colorado* magazine that won the 1999 Addy Award for best in-home publication with more than four colors.
- Created a sales and marketing product manual to delineate newspaper sections, ancillary products, and the demographics of the newspaper's core readership.
- Implemented the weekly *Peak Computing Magazine* from the ground up; responsible for product development and design, placement, distribution, setting advertising rates, sales, and creation of a companion web site.
- Collaborated with sister properties to develop "Living Well," a health tab special feature of the *Patriot Ledger.*
- Created an innovative research program for the *Times Advocate* (Team: Research) that provided the sales team with comprehensive and accurate demographic information to increase the effectiveness of client advertising.

Classified and Retail

- Directed retail sales to major, national, local, and automotive accounts of the *Patriot Ledger,* a daily newspaper with a circulation of 82,000.
- Directly supervised all commercial advertising sales functions for the *News-Chronicle* (a community newspaper with a circulation of 30,000), increasing revenues by 22%.
- Sold Pennysaver classified advertisements to commercial account advertisers.
- Increased gross sales by 131%, decreased new territory delinquencies by 40%, and achieved the top 10% of all sales executives.

Management and Supervision

- Developed and managed sales budgets of up to $17 million; accountable for print bids, production costs, and full profit and loss.
- Negotiated dollar volume contracts averaging $400,000, with highest being $1 million.
- Hired, trained, supervised, and mentored up to 5 managers and 45 staff members.
- Developed and negotiated a new commission plan for the *Patriot Ledger* retail department with union leaders.
- Managed production functions for the *Patriot Ledger* through prepress, including graphic design, copy input, page layout, and dispatch.

120

EXPERIENCE   *Management and Supervision (continued)*

- Contributed to the design and installation of an integrated advertising computer system that provides fully automated order entry, advertisement tracking, production, and pagination.
- Increased revenues for *Peak Computing* by 870% in 13 months and display advertisers by 400%, ultimately achieving $750,000 in annual sales.
- Managed the Porch Plus alternative delivery program for the *Times Advocate,* increasing revenues from $130,000 to $1.5 million.
- Collaborated with *The Orange County Register* to increase the market for Porch Plus.
- Served as co-chair of the San Diego North County Golf Expo, generating significant goodwill and $70,000 in new revenue.

Training

- Developed curriculum for and implemented a complete sales training program for all advertising associates of *The Gazette.*
- Wrote the company training manual for all departments.
- Conducted sales training seminars and created incentive programs.

HISTORY

PATRIOT LEDGER, Quincy, Massachusetts **Retail Advertising Director**	1999 – Present
THE GAZETTE, Colorado Springs, Colorado **Manager of Research and New Products** **Major Accounts/New Products Development Manager/Advertising Trainer** **Sales Manager for Peak Computing Magazine**	1995 – 1999 1999 1997 – 1999 1995 – 1997
TIMES ADVOCATE, Escondido, California **Marketing/Research Coordinator** **Retail Sales Manager for Porch Plus (Alternative Delivery Service)**	1994 – 1995
NEWS-CHRONICLE, Encinitas, California **Sales Manager (Retail and Classified)**	1993 – 1994
PENNYSAVER, San Diego, California **Classified Account Executive and Line Supervisor**	1990 – 1993

EDUCATION

BACHELOR OF ARTS, Material and Logistics Management **Michigan State University**, East Lansing, Michigan	1988

CONTINUING EDUCATION

Numerous leadership development training programs, including Legal Issues for Supervisors, Tactical Leadership (Hiring the Best, Performance Management, Documentation and Discipline, and Sexual Harassment), Train the Trainer, among others

PUBLICATION   Wrote and published an article in *Retail Insights* entitled "Customer Service" directed toward media advertising managers and directors.

121

TONY PACHECO

12 Anywhere Trail
Newtown, Colorado 81005

Phone: (719) 555-1234
E-mail: pacheco@protypeltd.com

PROFILE
- Experienced human resources manager with a diverse background in both manufacturing and high-tech services industries.
- Self-motivated professional with a strong work ethic and the ability to get the job done.
- Flexible quick learner who enjoys taking on new challenges and learning new processes.
- Known for the ability to bridge philosophies, build mutual trust, and create consensus.
- Bilingual—native English speaker, working knowledge of Spanish.
- Knowledge of Windows 95/98, MS Word, Excel, PowerPoint, Access, MS-Works, and e-mail.

AREAS OF EXPERTISE

Human Resource Regulations
- Safety Management/OSHA
- Wage and Hour/Wage Determinations
- State Laws/Federal Laws
- Service Contract/Davis-Bacon
- Employment/Labor Law/NLRB

Salary Administration
- Job Descriptions
- Standard Operating Procedures
- Position Evaluation
- Exempt/Nonexempt Pay
- Rate Ranges and Progression

Recruitment/Selection
- Executive/Administrative
- Nonexempt Hourly Sourcing
- Temporary Employment
- Outside Contractors
- Examination/Placement

Employee Relations
- EEOC/ADA/EEO-1 Reporting
- Affirmative Action Program Report
- Human Resources Auditor
- Corporate Advisor to the VP Services Dept.
- Federal Mediation and Conciliation
- Management Training of Contractual Intent
- Employee Relations Committee
- Negotiations Observer/Advisor
- Chief Contract Negotiator
- Grievance Handling/Steps I-II-III Arbitration
- Mutual Gains Bargaining Negotiations
- Arbitrator Selection
- Collective Bargaining (CBA)
- Arbitration Hearings (opening statement to end)

Benefits/Compensation
- 401k/Pensions/COBRA/WARN
- Workers' Compensation
- Loss Control

EXPERIENCE

HUMAN RESOURCES/LABOR RELATIONS MANAGER (1998 – present)
Mason and Hanger Corporation, Colorado Springs, Colorado
- Provide advice and counsel to managers and supervisors relating to human resource policies, procedures, and employee benefits for this military contractor with 400 employees in three sites.
- Listen to employee problems and provide feedback to functional managers to ensure that corrective action is taken.
- Discuss employee morale with site and program managers, indicating remedial action to resolve problem areas.
- Motivate and educate supervisors and manager to ensure consistent, equal, and fair treatment of all employees.
- Administer compensation and benefit programs, including insurance and 401K pension plans.
- Audit personnel records and maintain their security and confidentiality.
- Developed policies and procedures for exit interviews and ensured compliance with federal and state laws and regulations.
- Implemented an affirmative action program to meet federal requirements.
- Serve as a liaison between management and three unions.
- Negotiate and administer three collective bargaining agreements.
- Successfully increased trust between the union and the company, resulting in fewer filed grievances; saved more than half a million dollars by settling disputes without arbitration.
- Selected to diffuse a stalled bargaining agreement that had been referred for mediation with the Federal Mediation and Conciliation Board.
- Brought negotiations back on track and succeeded in negotiating a three-year contract in only four hours.

EXPERIENCE
(continued)

BUSINESS PROCESS TEAM MEMBER AND BUYER (1997 – 1998)
Colorado Fuel and Iron Corporation, Pueblo, Colorado
- Responsible for re-engineering departments and implementing process efficiencies.
- Rewrote job descriptions, combined jobs, and downsized operations of the tube mill, which saved $1 million a year in salaries, benefits, and production costs.
- Reorganized the Human Resources Department by outsourcing benefits administration to contractors, eliminating a vice president position and downsizing the department by two-thirds.
- Conducted task analyses, combined responsibilities for sales people, eliminated outside sales positions with extravagant perquisites, and instituted accountability measures to save more than $1 million per year.
- Made recommendations to hiring managers for staffing levels to meet production needs.
- Conducted performance evaluations of department managers and counseled them on areas needing improvement.
- Screened résumés, interviewed hundreds of workers, and made hiring recommendations to restaff the mill with non-union workers during an extended strike.
- Lowered the rejection rate of the rail mill by 7% through re-engineering of the dock to reduce damaged finished goods.
- As a buyer, sourced vendors and purchased more than $12 million in raw materials per month.
- Negotiated an across-the-board 10% decrease in prices from all vendors.
- Inventoried products received by rail and ensured that raw materials were received in time for production.

HUMAN RESOURCES/SAFETY COORDINATOR (1996)
Colorado Fuel and Iron Corporation, Pueblo, Colorado
- Implemented a $500,000 fall protection program for the steel mill that saved $4 million in noncompliance fines from OSHA.
- Conducted training classes on safety issues; developed drug and alcohol policies and procedures for the human resources department.

PRODUCTION WORKER (1993 – 1996)
Colorado Fuel and Iron Corporation, Pueblo, Colorado
- Financed a full undergraduate and graduate education as a laborer in this steel mill.
- Worked up the ladder to supervisor on the production floor of the Steel Making Department.

EDUCATION

MASTER OF BUSINESS ADMINISTRATION (1998)
Regis University, Denver, Colorado
- Emphasis in international business.
- Graduated in the top 15% of the graduating class.

BACHELOR OF ARTS DEGREE (1991)
Antioch University, George Meany Center for Labor Studies (AFL–CIO), Yellow Springs, Ohio
- Major in labor studies/labor relations.
- Completed 180 credit hours to graduate first in the class.
- Served as class president for two years.

LABOR CERTIFICATE (1989)
University of Colorado, Boulder
- Completed two six-week programs per year for a total of four years.

AFFILIATIONS

Member, Human Resources Association, Pueblo, Colorado
Member, Human Resources Association, Colorado Springs, Colorado
Member, National Society for Human Resource Management

COMMUNITY
SERVICE

Volunteer to teach and tutor adult students at the community college level in adult basic education, reading, literacy, and international business

LORETTA SCHWARTZ

PROFILE

- Focused retail manager with twenty years of experience.
- Background in marketing, sales, staff development, merchandising, and customer service.
- Effective team player with strong interpersonal and communication skills.
- Skilled in creating staff loyalty and empowering employees to excel.

EXPERIENCE

MANAGEMENT/ADMINISTRATION

- Directed the operations of 22 retail stores in three states with combined sales volume of $17.1 million.
- Served as a liaison between store management and home office merchandisers and senior managers.
- Approved sales goals and provided direction for floor sets (merchandising).
- Managed the daily operations of a high-volume retail clothing store; responsible for visual merchandising, floor supervision, and resolution of customer complaints and adjustments.
- Promoted from supervisor to manager of a $750,000 volume store and then to manager of a Casual Corner with more than $1 million in annual sales volume.
- Conceptualized and coordinated innovative fashion shows, breakfast clubs, and other promotions to increase sales volume and create customer loyalty.
- Developed new business through community involvement, seminars, and monthly training of sales staff to enhance customer service through the merchandise sales approach.

SUPERVISION/STAFF DEVELOPMENT

- Developed ten staff members for promotion to store manager or assistant store manager positions.
- Recruited, hired, trained, supervised, and evaluated sales associates, store supervisors, assistant managers, and store managers.
- Responsible for staff scheduling, ensuring adequate floor coverage, and overseeing payroll.

ACHIEVEMENTS

- Assumed responsibility for a failing district, closed unprofitable stores, and turned around declining units until all stores were profitable.
- Honored with membership in the Champions Club (1991–1992) for achieving #26 out of 860 stores in the country; Champions Club (1993–1994) achieving #48 out of 860 stores.
- Won numerous suit, dress, and pantyhose promotions by increasing sales over plan.
- Built sales volume through focused productivity training, visual merchandise presentation, and exceptional customer service.
- Voted President (1989–1990) and Vice President (1988) of the Towne East Square Merchants Association.
- President (1995–1996) and Vice President (1994) of Citadel Merchants Association.
- Selected as City Fashion Coordinator for Colorado Springs (1977–1978).
- Miss America Pageant Official (1977); First Runner Up, Miss Colorado Springs (1976).

WORK HISTORY

DISTRICT SALES MANAGER, Casual Corner, Denver, CO	1996 – Present
MANAGER, Casual Corner, Citadel Mall, Colorado Springs, CO	1990 – 1996
MANAGER, Casual Corner, Towne East, Wichita, KS	1982 – 1990
MANAGER, Casual Corner, Towne West, Wichita, KS	1981 – 1982

TRAINING

CASUAL CORNER CORPORATE TRAINING: TRAC I-III (Personal Selling, Beyond Customer Service, Driving the Business), MOHR Management Training

---

1445 Anywhere Court • Newtown, Colorado 80906 • (719) 555-1234

Sylvia Valley

4605 Anywhere Drive • Newtown, CO 80915 • Home (719) 555-1234 • Cell (719) 123-4567

PROFILE
- Versatile lyric soprano singer with more than twenty years of experience.
- Proven ability to sing in both solo and chorus performances.
- Background in classical, opera, sacred, and popular music.

EXPERIENCE

SOLO
- Douglas Moore's *Ballad of Baby Doe,* Samantha, Opera Theater of the Rockies, 2000
- Orff's *Carmina Burana,* soprano solos, Colorado Spring Children's Chorale and Youth Symphony, Dr. Anton Armstrong, Director, 2000
- Poulenc's *Gloria,* soprano solos, Soli Deo Gloria choir, Bob Crowder, Director, 1999
- Brahms' *Requiem,* soprano solo, Soli Deo Gloria choir, Edmund Ladouceur, Director, 1998
- Bach's *Magnificat,* "Quia Respexit," soprano solo, Soli Deo Gloria choir, Edmund Ladouceur, Director, 1997
- Vivaldi's *Gloria,* "Domine Deus," soprano solo, Soli Deo Gloria choir, Edmund Ladouceur, Director, 1996
- Sang the part of the youth from Mendelssohn's *Elijah* with the Soli Deo Gloria choir, Anna Hamre, Director, 1987
- Handel's *Messiah,* "He Shall Feed His Flock," Chapel Choir, Spangdahlem AFB, Germany, 1985
- Maria in *West Side Story,* College of Marin, Kentfield, California, May 1968
- Mendelssohn's *Oh for the Wings of a Dove,* College of Marin Madrigal group under the direction of Dr. S. Drummond Wolff, 1967
- Numerous solo performances with the College of Marin choir and Madrigal group under the direction of Dr. S. Drummond Wolff, 1966 – 1968
- Extensive solo experience performing at weddings and vocal recitals for many years

OPERA CHORUS
- *Pagliacci,* soprano, Opera Theater of the Rockies, 2001
- *La Boheme,* soprano, Colorado Opera Festival, 1998
- *Carmen,* soprano, Colorado Opera Festival, 1997
- *Lucia de Lammermoor,* second soprano, Colorado Opera Festival, 1996

CHORAL
- Eleven years of experience with Soli Deo Gloria Choir, Colorado Springs, directed by Anna Hamre and Edmund Ladouceur, 1987 – present
- Four years with the Abbey Singers, Colorado Springs, directed by Judy Wescott, 1996 – 2000
- Two years with the College of Marin choir and Madrigal group, Kentfield, California, 1966 – 1969

OTHER
- Sang a varied program of contemporary pop and 1930s/40s music for a Democratic party fund raiser, Idara Productions International, 1997
- Sang wedding songs and Bach Gounod *Ave Maria* for an Idara Productions International bridal fashion show at the Red Lion Inn, Colorado Springs, 1996

MUSIC TRAINING

COLLEGE OF MARIN, Kentfield, California, 1966 – 1969
- Two years as a music major, acquiring 62 credits toward a Bachelor of Arts degree

VOICE TRAINING
- Pat Staubo, Colorado Springs, Colorado, 1997 – present
- Connie Heidenreich, Colorado Springs, Colorado, 1989 – 1991
- Marion Marsh, San Rafael, California, 1966 – 1968
- Madam Resick, Mill Valley, California, 1964 – 1966

LARRY D. SISK

3480 Hoofprint Road
Peyton, Colorado 80831

Telephone:
(719) 683-7522

PROFILE
- Seasoned construction superintendent with a comprehensive knowledge of the business and more than 30 years of experience in:
  - Commercial and residential building
  - New construction and renovations
  - Bid preparation and contract negotiations
  - Surveying
  - Job scheduling
  - Blueprint specifications
- Effective leader who is able to motivate employees and subcontractors to complete jobs on time.
- Skilled at evaluating margins to ensure profitability at project completion
- Proven ability to complete projects on time and under budget.

SUMMARY
- Supervised large commercial construction projects from bid through final walk-through.
- Responsible for project takeoffs, estimating, and development of project schedules and milestones.
- Sourced vendors, purchased supplies and equipment, and ensured timely delivery of materials.
- Evaluated blueprints and schematics; ensured compliance with regulations and specifications.
- Consulted with clients regarding design modifications and change orders; ensured customer satisfaction throughout the project life cycle
- Interviewed, hired, scheduled, and supervised employees and subcontractors.
- Evaluated bids from subcontractors, ensured the quality of their work, and resolved problems.
- Implemented safety and quality control programs and regulations.
- As a business owner, was accountable for long-range planning, profit and loss, controlling costs, invoicing, recordkeeping, collecting accounts receivable, and monitoring financial performance.

SIGNIFICANT PROJECTS
- Biggs Kofford, CPA, Office Addition, $1.2 million (2002)
- Lake Point Medical Center, Design/Build Medical Office Building, $4.5 million (2000 – 2001)
- Falcon School District, Classroom Remodels, Gymnasium Additions, $1.9 million (1999 – 2000)
- Summit County Jail, New Detention Facility, Breckenridge, $7.5 million (1990)
- Santa Fe County Jail, New Detention Facility, Santa Fe, New Mexico, $8 million (1989)
- Evans Army Hospital, New Facility, Fort Carson, $95 million (1984)
- ADAL Computer Center, New Computer Facility, USAF Academy, $2.5 million (1983)
- Nixon Power and Sewage Disposal Plant, City Utility Project, $20 million (1979)
- American Numismatic Building, New Corporate Headquarters Building, $1.5 million (1978)
- Doherty High School, New Facility, $14 million (1975 – 1976)
- First Bank, New Building, $12 million (1974)

EXPERIENCE
Superintendent, Classic General Contractors, Colorado Springs, Colorado (1999 – present)
Estimator, BMC West, Colorado Springs, Colorado (1999)
Owner/Manager, Bulldog Construction, Peyton, Colorado (1988 – 1999)
Journeyman Carpenter, AA Construction, Colorado Springs, Colorado (1987 – 1988)
Journeyman Carpenter, Robert E. McKee Construction Company, Denver, Colorado (1986 – 1987)
Journeyman Carpenter, Desman Corporation (Chapman), Colorado Springs, Colorado (1986 – 1987)
Cement Finisher, Transco Pacific Company, Fort Carson, Colorado (1986)
Superintendent, Hibbitts Construction Company, Colorado Springs, Colorado (1986)
Carpenter Foreman, Sommers Building Company, Colorado Springs, Colorado (1986)
Journeyman Carpenter, Alvarado Construction Company, Denver, Colorado (1985 – 1986)
Ironworker, Bates Construction Company, Colorado Springs, Colorado (1985)
Superintendent, H.W. Houston Construction Company, Pueblo, Colorado (1984 – 1985)
Carpenter Foreman, McNally Construction Company, Colorado Springs, Colorado (1984)

EDUCATION
JOURNEYMAN CARPENTER, Southern Colorado State College, Pueblo, Colorado (1968 – 1971)
Completed a four-year carpenter apprenticeship program under the Carpenters and Joiners of America Local 515, Pueblo, Colorado

MILD STEEL ARC WELDER, Pikes Peak Community College, Colorado Springs, Colorado (1971)

Paragraph Style or Bullets

Good advertisements are designed in such a way that the reader's eye is immediately drawn to important pieces of information using type and graphic elements, including bold, italics, headline fonts, and so forth. Then the design must guide the reader's eye down the page from one piece of information to the next with the judicious use of white space or graphic lines.

In this science of typography, very long lines of text (longer than six or seven inches, depending on the font) and large blocks of text (more than seven typeset lines) are considered to be tiring to the reader's eye. If you look closely at textbooks, magazines, and newspapers, you will notice that the information is usually typeset in columns to reduce line lengths, and journalists intentionally write in short paragraphs because they are more reader-friendly.

How does this science translate into a résumé? As a general rule, you should keep your lines of text no longer than seven inches—five to six inches is even better—and your paragraphs shorter than seven lines of text each. Many people find it difficult to cram the description of a job and its accomplishments into a single paragraph while following this rule. Therefore, you will often see bulleted sentences used instead of paragraphs on résumés.

If you prefer the paragraph style, there are some tricks of the trade that can help make your résumé more readable:

1. List the job summary in paragraph form and then use bullets to highlight your achievements.

Provost and Dean of Faculties, Hofstra University . . . . 1990 – Present
Interim Provost and Dean of Faculties, Hofstra University . . . . 1989 – 1990
In a position second only to the President of the University, the Provost is responsible for the entire academic area of the University, including all of the Colleges and Schools, Libraries, Honors Program, Center for Teaching Excellence, Computer Center, Scott Skodnek Business Development Center, and the Joan and Arnold Saltzman Community Services Center. Accountable for developing and managing an annual budget of $80+ million.

- *Successfully negotiated two five-year contracts with the University faculty* (1991–1996, 1996–2001) as the chief negotiator. Completed negotiations three months before the expiration of the existing contracts. The first five-year contract resulted in a nine-hour teaching load for faculty at a manageable economic cost to the University. The present contract has a unique incentive plan to promote early retirement, and the contract also provides compensation increases that are tied, in part, to the well-being of the University.

- *Currently leading the efforts to establish the Honors College,* which is a key aspect of our strategy for the future and an important factor in tailoring the profile of the entire class. The Honors College builds on the existing Honors Program and will be open to all qualified undergraduate students regardless of their major.

2. Divide your experience into related information and use several shorter paragraphs under each job description.

EXPERIENCE

EXECUTIVE DIRECTOR OF ASSESSMENT (May 2002 – present)
Colorado Springs School District 11, Colorado Springs, Colorado
Direct all operations related to research, planning, assessment, evaluation, technology integration, and technology support for every school in the district (elementary, middle/senior high, and charter schools). Participate in the development of long-range strategic plans for the district and the department. Develop assessment methodology, reporting systems, and related utilization of technology.

Serve as a liaison between the Research Center of the University of Colorado at Colorado Springs and District 11's Board of Education. Develop and lead the Coordination Committee responsible for bringing IT and Instruction together on a district level. Oversee the Evaluation Unit that monitors district programs, task forces, and initiatives. Meet weekly with instructional services to align technology integration and assessment with the needs of literacy resource teachers and instructional specialists.

Accomplishments

Significantly revitalized the Assessment Unit by improving communication and implementing changes based on feedback from performance measurements. Personally conducted teacher telephone surveys throughout the year to evaluate service delivery. Piloted the concept of Building Assessment Teams to promote better utilization of assessment data. Improved service delivery by aligning the work of technical support, network administration, and the call center.

Fiscal Responsibility

Set budget priorities for two units; accountable for a total of $2.5 million in district funds. Actively campaigned for the 2002 bond issue.

3. Use left headings instead of centered headings to make the line lengths shorter (like in the sample above). This won't work, however, when the shorter line length forces your information into very long paragraphs. It is better to have longer line lengths and shorter paragraphs.

Bullets are by far my most favorite way of presenting information on a résumé. Bullets are special characters (• ✦ ▪) used at the beginning of indented short sentences to call attention to individual items on a résumé. Short, bulleted sentences are easier to read than long paragraphs of text, and they highlight the information you want the reader to see quickly. Bullets also add some variety to a résumé and make it just a touch more creative.

In both MS Word and WordPerfect for Windows or Macintosh, clicking on "Insert" gives you access to a myriad of special characters that are not found on your keyboard.

On the following pages are sample résumés designed using paragraph formats, bulleted styles, and combinations thereof.

128

Sean M. Michaels

4533 Anywhere Drive • Newtown, Colorado 80918 • (719) 555-1234 • E-mail: seda@protypeltd.com

PROFILE
- Dependable system administrator with more than four years of experience.
- Proven troubleshooter who gets to the root of the problem quickly.
- Known for being able to see the big picture without getting lost in the details.
- Effective team leader with strong communication and interpersonal skills.
- Hold a current secret security clearance.

TECHNOLOGY

Networks: Microsoft Certified Systems Engineer (MCSE), Windows 2000, #2306869

Operating Systems: Windows 95/98/2000/NT 4.0

Applications: MS Word, Excel, PowerPoint, Access, Outlook, Internet Explorer, MS Project, Front-Page, Terminal Services, Document Management Extensions (DME), Ghost Utility, Procurement Desktop (PD^2), Defense Messaging System (DMS), VisioTech, VisioPro, Automated Business Service System, and various government financial applications (IAPS, PBAS, InfoConnect, JOCAS II)

EXPERIENCE

SYSTEM ADMINISTRATOR, L-3 Communications, Schriever AFB, Colorado (1998 – present)
Provide system administration support for a large research and development network with 1,200 computers and 900 users. Install, maintain, and troubleshoot NT 4.0 and Windows 2000 workstations, laptops, and peripherals (printers, scanners, CD-RW drives, JAZ and ZIP backups, etc.). Lead a team of 20 technicians on various engineering change projects. Provide technical expertise to all personnel within the organization.

Hardware Experience:
- Troubleshoot hardware failures and resolve hardware conflicts (IDE and SCSI).
- Install peripherals and upgrade hardware on desktop workstations.
- Design and install workgroups networks: run cabling, configure ports and network protocols, add accounts to the domain, and verify connectivity.

Software Experience:
- Install Windows-based operating systems and applications on a 2,000-node Ethernet network.
- Configure workstations for WAN/LAN network connectivity.
- Install, configure, maintain, and optimize software applications and resolve conflicts.
- Engineered the Windows 2000 upgrade and interoperability with the NT 4.0 environment.
- Provide user support for MS Office and industry-specific applications.

CABLE INSTALLATION TECHNICIAN, Superior Design, Schriever AFB, Colorado (1998)
Assigned to Schriever by a temporary staffing firm. Surveyed, planned, and led installation teams on various cable engineering projects. Installed and terminated category 5 and fiber optic cable for up to 400 workstations per job. Interpreted cable trace schematics, subflooring and ceiling blueprints, power diagrams, and cable tray layouts. Accountable for equipment, installation tools, and cable materials.

SENIOR MEDICAL SERGEANT (E-6), U.S. Army, Fort Carson, Colorado (1988 – 1998)
Managed all medical care, training, and readiness for an operational detachment. Ordered and inventoried medical equipment and supplies valued at more than $40,000. Ensured that all team members were medically ready for deployment to foreign countries, including immunizations and medical records. Established mobile satellite communications as an air defense artillery missile crewman for three years before cross-training into the medical field.

EDUCATION

BACHELOR OF SCIENCE IN INFORMATION TECHNOLOGY
Colorado Technical University, Colorado Springs, Colorado (2001 – present)
University of Colorado, Colorado Springs, Colorado (2000)
Pikes Peak Community College, Colorado Springs, Colorado (1998 – 2000)
- Currently one year from completion of the degree
- Relevant course work completed: C++ Programming, Database Applications, Introduction to Networking, Client/Server Systems and Network Administration, Client/Server Operating System NT

MICHAEL T. SIMS, CPA

PROFILE

- Results-oriented financial management professional with solid experience in the telecommunications industry.
- Certified Public Accountant with more than 12 years of Fortune 100 corporate strategic planning, financial analysis, reporting, accounting, and auditing experience.
- Graduate of the prestigious Thunderbird Executive Program (International MBA).
- Extensive international business experienced throughout Asia, Europe, Mexico, and Canada.

STRENGTHS

- Strategic planning, management consulting, business support, process improvement, superior customer service, financial analysis, reporting, auditing, accounting, and budgets.
- Highly organized change agent with the ability to implement innovative ideas to achieve positive solutions.
- Decision maker with the commitment to create a climate for success and the ability to bring order to chaos.
- Team leader who is able to motivate others toward achievement of an organization's vision and goals.
- Effective trainer and coach, able to present concepts clearly to all audiences—from entry-level staff to CEOs.

Financial

- Financial planning and forecasting experience in all aspects of corporate finance, including cost centers, employee benefits, new business proposals, and revenue accounting.
- Skilled in the re-engineering of business accounting processes to streamline reporting procedures.
- Experienced in spreadsheet modeling of corporate financial statements, including income statements, cash flow statements, and balance sheets.
- Background in cross-functional operations of management, marketing, research and development, information technology, manufacturing, and human resources.

Technology

- Macro understanding of three converging industries: telecommunications, computers, and cable television.
- Proficient in the use of numerous computer applications and operating systems, including Windows, DOS, Lotus, Excel, MS Word, WordPerfect, PowerPoint, Office 95, communications (Netscape, Internet, Dow Jones News Retrieval, America Online, CompuServe, Easytriev, RAMIS), Lotus Notes, etc.

PROFESSIONAL EXPERIENCE

AG COMMUNICATION SYSTEMS *(A joint venture of AT&T and GTE),* Phoenix, Arizona (1984 – Present)
Financial Benefits Specialist (January 1996 – Present)
Manager of employee benefits accounting and finance for this $310 million company involved in the development, manufacture, and marketing of software for the telecommunications industry. Full responsibility for the management of $400 million in corporate benefit plan assets. Prepare annual budgets, quarterly forecasts, and long-range plans for all benefits and executive compensation programs, including health, 401K, savings, and pension plans. Ensure accurate financial accounting of the defined benefit and contribution plans, as well as compliance with all federal tax and regulatory plan filings.

- Lead finance support for employee benefit design activities, including transition to flexible benefits, selection of healthcare providers, implementation of a cash balance pension plan, and 401K changes.
- Enhanced the major forecasting processes for $45 million of annual employee benefits and compensation.
- Improved communications and trust between benefits department and primary customer, controller, treasurer, financial planning and analysis, external auditors, pension trustee, and medical consultants.

Manager of Business Analysis and Planning, Senior Financial Analyst (July 1991 – January 1996)
Supervised the financial management of the Network Services Division with $43 million in sales, $3 million in services inventory, and a staff of 500. Responsible for the forecasting, reporting, and analysis of sales, direct costs, period costs, and services inventory. Involved in the preparation of the annual budget and salary plan, rolling annual forecast, five-year business plan, and reconciliations of actual to target.

- Relocated business planning and analysis function from Illinois to Arizona and reduced staff by one-third to realize $80,000 in annual cost savings.
- Introduced and implemented streamlined reporting procedures, significantly improving presentation of financial information to senior management.

ADDRESS

6734 West Anywhere Avenue, Newtown, Arizona 85308-5505
(602) 555-1234

PROFESSIONAL EXPERIENCE

AG COMMUNICATION SYSTEMS (continued)
Continuation: Manager of Business Analysis and Planning, Senior Financial Analyst

- Converted $16 million of revenue recognition and $6 million of inventory accounting from manual to computerized processing.
- Simplified accounting and planning processes, improving reporting and saving $400,000 annually.
- Created a monthly sales through margin report which uncovered $2.7 million in cost overstatements.
- Set up and maintained monthly financial reporting and forecasting controls for $20 million in software sales.
- Prepared balance sheet and cash flow statement for the 1994 – 1998 business plan.

Special Projects: Responsible for diverse special projects, including the financial planning, analysis, and reporting treatment for software accounting and hardware warranty reserves, restatement of the 1994 budget, finance benchmarking, and the creation of finance key indicators. Lead support person in financial planning, analysis, and reporting for the research and development/product development organization. Served as financial representative on a special two-month project in the research and development of a business plan for the startup of a new wireless business.

- Researched and prepared business case analysis and financial statements, including pro-formas, net present values, and internal rate of returns calculations to determine revenue requirements for business startup.
- Introduced accounting policy changes regarding revenue recognition, software accounting methodologies, and hardware warranty reserves.
- Reduced financial support costs by $100,000 for 1994 through improvements to the financial planning, analysis, and reporting of the company's $49 million R&D cost center.
- Recommended that all R&D labor be consolidated from 30 different departments into one department to simplify planning, reporting, and analysis.
- Successfully reduced closing cycle by 25% as acting manager of general accounting and financial planning.
- Administered and facilitated the change from a micro- to a macro-based total company budget for 1995.
- Participated in the creation of the company's three strategic quality initiatives as finance representative on a cross-functional Quality Focus Team.
- Upgraded financial management to Microsoft Excel and Windows environments.

Marketing Financial Analyst, Supervisor of Accounting Operations/Services, Senior Financial Analyst, Financial Analyst, Staff Auditor/Senior Auditor (1984 – 1991)
Consolidated the sales and margin financial plans and monthly actual reporting. Directly forecasted $160 million of sales and presented monthly actual results, forecast, and variance data to VP of Marketing. Maintained and controlled the general ledger system and established the new general ledger for the joint venture between GTE and AT&T. Prepared quarterly SEC reporting to GTE. Served as member of the Finance Quality Committee.

- Implemented the first local area network in finance which improved departmental efficiency and accuracy.
- Reduced the number of records in the new joint venture general ledger by 75%.

ESMARK, INC., Chicago, Illinois (1983 – 1984)
Staff Auditor: Performed compliance audits to support Arthur Young's data on year-end financial statements.

EDUCATION

MASTER OF INTERNATIONAL MANAGEMENT—EXECUTIVE PROGRAM (1995)
American Graduate School of International Management, Thunderbird, Glendale, Arizona

BACHELOR OF SCIENCE IN ACCOUNTING (1983)
Northern Illinois University, Dekalb, Illinois

CONTINUING EDUCATION: Committed to life-long learning and self-development. Attended lectures by Tom Peters and former British Prime Minister Margaret Thatcher. Attended Dr. Deming's Quality Seminar, Dale Carnegie's Effective Public Speaking and Human Relations workshops, and seminars on employee benefits sponsored by the American Institute for International Research and the American Institute of Certified Public Accountants. Participated in GTE 3-5 day training programs on risk analysis, forecasting and strategy, financial analysis, and managing for results.

131

Executive Résumés

Webster defines an executive as "a person whose function is to administer or manage affairs of a corporation, division, department, group of companies, etc." This can be the president, director, chief executive officer, chief financial officer, chief information officer, controller, executive director, vice president, general manager, treasurer, principal, owner, and the list goes on.

Generally, a person in such a position has strategically worked his/her way to the top echelons of management over a period of at least ten years. Executives tend to have many relevant past positions, credentials, achievements, published articles, speaking engagements, community service activities, or other important qualifications.

In order to reflect this experience, an executive résumé is almost always more than one page. In fact, an executive résumé can be as long as it needs to be in order to convince the reader that the candidate has what it takes to manage an organization effectively.

Just because an executive résumé is long, however, doesn't mean it should be wordy. The same good writing described in Chapter 9 is even more important in an executive résumé. Because the number of applicants for an executive position is generally not as large as for lower-level positions, every word of an executive's résumé will be read many times before a decision is made. Make sure every word you write serves a purpose!

On the next page is an example of an effective executive résumé.

DAVID A. SMITH, JD, LL.M., CPA

5797 South Anywhere Street • Newtown, Colorado 80111
Home: (720) 555-1234 • Cellular: (720) 123-4567 • E-mail: dsmith@protypeltd.com

EXECUTIVE SUMMARY

Chief Financial Officer and Strategic Business Executive with 15+ years of proven achievement driving solid revenue and bottom-line gains through expert financial, legal, and operational contributions to merger and acquisition transactions, new business development, turnaround operations, and high-growth ventures. Quantifiable results in the areas of:

Negotiations • Board/Investor Relations • Effective Communications
Cost Containment • Integration Planning • Results Analysis • System Conversions/Upgrades
Public/Private Infusions • Equity/Debt Financings • Financial Reporting

Aggressive, results-focused, strategic leader offering a unique blend of operations, financial, and legal expertise producing significant financial gains and meeting operational objectives. Led dynamic growth and expansion efforts for investments of Goldman Sachs and other investment firms. Championed bankruptcy workouts and business turnarounds. Full P&L responsibility for multiple divisions in multi-million-dollar organizations. Intrinsic leadership skills fostering top performance and efficiency through team-focused strategies.

PROFESSIONAL EXPERIENCE AND ACHIEVEMENTS

VICE PRESIDENT, LEGAL AND BUSINESS SERVICES (2000 – present)
Coram Healthcare Corporation, Denver, Colorado

Spearheaded aggressive financial, legal, and operational turnaround for the nation's second largest supplier of infusion therapies. Streamlined and maximized budgetary accountability for $75 million in legal affairs, merger and acquisition activities, business development, SEC reporting, human resources, compliance, risk management, and administrative departments.

- Achieved and surpassed investor EBITDA and capital/debt restructuring goals.
- Initiated, negotiated, and closed $230+ million of capital restructurings at critical stages of the bankruptcy workout.
- Delivered a 23% EBITDA increase through combined M&A revenue enhancements and cost reductions.
- Enhanced cash flow 13% and contribution margins 9% by restructuring multiple departments for improved efficiencies.
- Infused business with $41.5 million cash by leading divestiture of non-accretive divisions.
- Negotiated a successful $18+ million resolution of $28+ million in tax liens.
- Produced 7% shift in core business and revenue quality through trend analysis and deployment of a benchmarking financial model to branch operations.

SVP BUSINESS AND LEGAL AFFAIRS / CHIEF FINANCIAL OFFICER (1998 – 2000)
ExchangeBridge.com, Atlanta, Georgia

Achieved financial, legal, and operational goals for this telecommunications e-business startup. Raised venture capital and implemented core business strategies focusing on cash flow, M&A activities, return on investments, business line mix, and same-store EBITDA levels. Led business development initiatives for an aggressive marketing strategy that created new distribution channels for product lines.

- Strengthened cash position by leading $75+ million in business development efforts and divestiture of multiple web sites and by transferring intellectual property for publishing and pharmacy-based businesses.
- Accelerated return on investment from 3.6% to more than 28%, dramatically exceeding investor goals and building momentum for the eventual sale of the company to a strategic partner with full payout to investors.
- Brought the company from the brink of bankruptcy by structuring the workout of payroll tax liens, realigning staff functions, and negotiating favorable arrangements with vendors.

133

- Raised financings for senior and subordinated mezzanine debt restructurings required for merger of an insurance-based business utilizing discounted cash flow valuable analysis.
- Championed five-fold increase in EBITDA, 20% improvement in receivable collections, and 33% enhancement of inventory turns, achieving business turnaround despite rapidly decreasing cash flows (high growth, low margins) and culminating in a profitable exit event for investors.
- Ensured SEC compliance and registration of an IPO offering. Minimized operational challenges associated with post-closing integrations by consolidating all due diligence efforts.

SENIOR VICE PRESIDENT, FINANCIAL AND LEGAL AFFAIRS / GENERAL COUNSEL (1992 – 1998)
Meridian Corporation, Memphis, Tennessee

Led team efforts for expansion and integration planning, including consolidation of financial, operational, and administrative functions for the nation's largest home healthcare company with 12,000+ employees and $500+ million in revenues. Negotiated and closed 75+ M&A transactions for management services divisions, producing debt/equity infusions. Consolidated $50+ million budgetary responsibility for financial services, marketing, legal, back office, and administrative departments.

- Spearheaded strategic three-year expansion for 350+ locations in 34 states and three countries by developing effective M&A growth strategies, leading due diligence, and reducing integration timelines to less than 150 days.
- Orchestrated $500+ million industry consolidation/merger through negotiations with industry leaders and alignment of investor and shareholder objectives.
- Reduced costs 15% by introducing stringent resource management and budgeting policies, reorganizing the sales force, and eliminating unproductive administrative support functions.
- Negotiated and closed $250 million syndicated debt restructuring and $85 million equity capitalizations.
- Decreased Medicare denials 13+% as chair of the Compliance and Risk Management Committees with rollout of improved financial reporting guidelines to all branch operations.
- Led successful integration of financial and telecommunications arrangements across more than 200 locations.

SENIOR ASSOCIATE / FIRST-LEVEL PARTNER (1990 – 1992)
McDonnell Boyd, LLC, Memphis, Tennessee

Directed and implemented complex capital/debt financings and restructurings, consolidations, divestitures, public and private stock placements, and M&A transactions. Provided counsel and led legal compliance initiatives, litigation strategies, executive compensation, and intellectual property and employment law issues. Furthered SEC reporting experience.

- Piloted $250+ million merger of hospital chains involving complex bond restructuring requirements.
- Charted a successful $50+ million expansion of Canadian and Latin American transportation business lines.
- Structured and navigated workout of a commercial carrier logistics-based company.

SENIOR ASSOCIATE (1988 – 1990)
Allen & Scruggs, LLC, Memphis, Tennessee

Directed commercial litigation, securitizations, SEC filings, and healthcare issues. Negotiated and consummated commercial, tax, and M&A arrangements, offerings, compliance, and intellectual property issues. Represented clients before federal and state courts and regulatory agencies.

- Maneuvered negotiations and closing for a $25+ million nationwide franchising program.
- Managed troubled debt restructurings and bankruptcy court filings for multiple clients.
- Drafted $100+ million multinational purchase/sales export agreements for expansion of business lines into Japan, Mexico, and Latin America.

EDUCATION

LL.M. IN TAXATION (1988)
Washington University School of Law, St. Louis, Missouri

JURIS DOCTOR (1985)
University of Memphis School of Law, Memphis, Tennessee

BACHELOR OF ARTS, PSYCHOLOGY AND ACCOUNTING (1982)
Christian Brothers University, Memphis, Tennessee

AFFILIATIONS AND PUBLICATIONS

Certified Public Accountant   1989, 250+ hours Continuing Education Units (CEU)

Tennessee Bar Association   1985 – 2001, Young Lawyers Division, Chairman of Child Waiting Room Project, Chairman of Oversight Committee, ADR Section

Author   "Keeping the Secret in Trade Secrets," (April 1997), *ACCA Magazine*

Speaker   Financial Statements for Nonfinancial Attorneys, Trade Secret Protection, M&A Planning, Integration Activities and Timelines: Application Service Provider Issues and Practical Solutions

Community Relations   Homeowners Association, First Vice President (2001 – 2002)
Chaired homeowners committee of county government board (1998 – 1999)
United Way representative (1995 – 1997)
Child Witness Waiting Room, county government liaison (1995 – 1996)
Big Brothers representative (1992 – 1995)

Curriculum Vitae

Remember when I said there is an exception to every rule in the résumé business? Well, here's another one. In most cases, résumés should be concise and limited to one or two pages at the most. You will carefully select your information to provide a synopsis. In some professions, however, a much longer résumé is expected and the longer the résumé, the better your chances of getting an interview.

Those industries generally include medicine, law, education, science, and media (television, film, etc.). If you are applying for a job in a foreign country, long résumés with more detail and a considerable amount of personal information are the norm.

Such a professional résumé is called a *curriculum vita* (CV) from the Latin meaning "course of one's life" (literally like running a race—and you just *thought* your life was a rat race!). For those of us who have trouble knowing how to spell the word, *vita* is singular and *vitae* is plural.

A successful CV will include not only education and experience but also:

• publications (books, magazines, journals, and other media)

• certifications and licenses

• grants and research

• professional affiliations

• awards and honors

• presentations, and/or courses taught

Anything relevant to your industry is appropriate to use on a CV, and the résumé can be as long as it needs to be to present the "course of your life."

A CV—or any résumé with multiple pages for that matter—must contain a header with your name and page number on each successive page. Should the pages become separated, the reader should be able to easily put your subsequent pages in their proper order and with *your* résumé!

Let's take a look at a sample CV.

CAROL S. KLEINMAN, Ph.D., R.N.

PROFILE

- Experienced university professor and academic administrator.
- Able to bring real-world nursing and healthcare administration experience to the classroom.
- Effective team player with strong communication and interpersonal skills.
- Known for dynamic presentation style and the ability to reach any student.

TEACHING EXPERIENCE

ASSOCIATE PROFESSOR (1999 – Present)
College of Nursing, Seton Hall University, South Orange, New Jersey
- Developed and delivered the first completely online College of Nursing course in multimedia format—"Theoretical Basis of Advanced Practice Nursing."
- Teach graduate courses in nursing and health services administration.

ADJUNCT CLINICAL PROFESSOR (1999 – Present)
Department of Nursing, Essex County College, Newark, New Jersey
- Guide undergraduate students through clinical rotations in psychiatry.

PROFESSOR OF GRADUATE NURSING (1997 – 1999)
Clarkson College, Omaha, Nebraska
- Taught selected courses in health services administration, all courses in the nursing administration major, and core courses in graduate nursing curricula.
- Consistently received among the highest student reviews of all the faculty in the college.

ADJUNCT PROFESSOR (1993 – 1997)
School of Nursing, Barry University, Miami, Florida
- Taught core courses in the graduate nursing curriculum.

ASSISTANT PROFESSOR AND COURSE COORDINATOR (1978 – 1986)
School of Nursing, City College of New York
- Coordinated teaching team in upper junior level integrated nursing course.
- Taught all psychiatric content throughout the undergraduate nursing curriculum, including clinical teaching in psychiatric inpatient settings.
- Member of the Course and Standing Committee; Chair of the Evaluation Committee; Member of the Community Mental Health Liaison Committee.

COURSES TAUGHT

GRADUATE NURSING COURSES:
- Nursing Theories and Concept Development
- Theories and Concepts of Advanced Nursing Practice
- Nursing Research
- Nursing Theory
- Social Context of Healthcare
- Theories and Concepts of Nursing Administration
- Psychosocial Assessment and Intervention in Primary Care
- Thesis Development

GRADUATE HEALTH SERVICES ADMINISTRATION COURSES:
- Operations Management
- Organizational Theory and Behavior
- Human Resources Management
- Reimbursement and Managed Care
- Forces in Healthcare
- Thesis Development

GRANTS AND RESEARCH

- Health and Human Services, Division of Nursing, Online MSN/MBA, December 2001.
- Health and Human Services, Division of Nursing, Online MSN, Health Systems Administration, December 2001.
- Developed research proposal for "Leadership styles and staff nurse retention" approved for implementation at Clara Maass Medical Center.

ADDRESS

18 Anywhere Court, Anytown, NJ 07747, Phone: (732) 555-1234, E-mail: drcsk@protypeltd.com

EDUCATION

CERTIFICATES
Imago Relationship Therapy, Institute for Imago Relationship Therapy (1991)
Clinical Fellowship in Hypnotherapy, Morton Prince Center for Hypnosis (1979)

Ph.D., BEHAVIORAL SCIENCE, Specialization in Psychotherapy (1983)
Florida Institute of Technology, School of Professional Psychology
- Dissertation: "Attitudes Toward Mental Illness by Student Nurses from Various Ethnic Groups"
- Honors: Graduate Assistantship (2 years)

MASTER OF SCIENCE, Psychiatric-Mental Health Nursing (1975)
Adelphi University, School of Nursing
- Thesis: "A Conceptual Model of Female Homosexuality from the Perspective of Analytical Psychology"
- Honors: NIMH Traineeship for Graduate Study, Sigma Theta Tau

BACHELOR OF SCIENCE IN NURSING, Major in Psychiatric Nursing (1973)
State University of New York at Stony Brook
- Honors: Graduated cum laude

ASSOCIATE OF APPLIED SCIENCE IN NURSING (1971)
Kingsborough Community College, City University of New York
- Honors: Salutatorian (third in a class of 1,000), Phi Theta Kappa, Dean's List, President's Award, Department of Nursing Award

ADMINISTRATIVE EXPERIENCE

DIRECTOR, NURSING ADMINISTRATION PROGRAM (1999 – Present)
Seton Hall University, South Orange, New Jersey
- Developed a dual degree program with the Stillman School of Business offering an MSN/MBA as a collaborative degree program.
- Created a Master of Nursing Education program offered completely online through SetonWorld-Wide, the virtual university branch of Seton Hall.
- Completed a comprehensive revision of the Master of Science in Nursing Case Management program.
- Developed a grant proposal to obtain federal funding for the Nursing Administration graduate program.

DIRECTOR, HEALTH SERVICES ADMINISTRATION (1997 – 1999)
Nebraska Health Services, Omaha, Nebraska
- Directed the graduate program in Health Services Administration; responsible for operations management, budgeting, curriculum design, faculty supervision, and student recruitment initiatives.
- Developed and implemented a complete redesign of the curriculum based on market analysis.
- Involved in developing innovative new Internet-based distance learning programs.
- Created a program that allowed students to obtain dual graduate degrees.
- Developed incentives and interfaces between the undergraduate and graduate programs of the college to prevent loss of graduate students to competitive schools.
- Member of the Heartland Healthcare Executive Group; revitalized this regional chapter of the American College of Healthcare Executives, developed relationships with healthcare leaders in the community, and served as faculty advisor.

DIRECTOR, BEHAVIORAL HEALTH SERVICES (1993 – 1996)
Broward General Medical Center, Ft. Lauderdale, Florida
- Responsible for the administrative and clinical management of the behavioral health department of the fourth largest integrated health care delivery system in the nation.
- Directed the 98-bed inpatient service, crisis stabilization unit, psychiatric emergency services, specialty treatment unit, and mental health initiatives within primary health centers.
- Developed a consultation and liaison service to trauma and other hospital departments.
- Managed an expense budget of more than $7 million and a staff of 135 FTEs.
- Developed a re-engineering plan that modernized the care delivery model and restaffed the department, saving $400,000 a year in salary and benefit expenses.
- Absorbed all of the county mental health services valued at $4 million.
- Rewrote the department's policy and procedure manual; implemented a new quality assurance program.

EXPERIENCE
(continued)

EXECUTIVE DIRECTOR (1992 – 1993)
American Day Treatment Centers of Miami, Florida

- Directed all administrative and clinical operations of a freestanding, for-profit center that provided adult, adolescent, and geriatric partial hospitalization programs.
- Developed this new program from the ground up, including definition and marketing of products, programs, and services.
- Responsible for managing the construction project, purchasing capital equipment, and staffing.
- Administered a $2 million budget, achieving profitability within twelve months.

DIRECTOR, OUTPATIENT SERVICES (1986 – 1992)
Green Oaks Psychiatric Hospital, Dallas, Texas

- Created and directed the outpatient department of a 106-bed psychiatric hospital, including adult, adolescent, and chemical dependency partial hospitalization programs.
- Developed and implemented programs and services, making them profitable in less than a year.
- Grew the program to 25 staff members in a dedicated 10,000 sq. ft. office space with a $2 million budget and 50 patients per day.
- Responsible for strategic planning, marketing, referral development, and regulatory compliance.
- Elected to the national Board of Directors of the Association for Ambulatory Behavioral Healthcare.

SELECTED
PRESENTATIONS

- Business and Health Administration Association Conference, Chicago, Illinois, February 28, 2002.
- "Education for future nurse leaders." Keynote presentation for the Council of School Presidents, New Jersey Nursing Students, Inc., November 2002.
- "Education for nurse leaders of the future." New Jersey State Nurses Association, Atlantic City, New Jersey, April 2001.
- "Roles, power, and opportunities for men in nursing." American Assembly of Men in Nursing, Seattle, Washington, December 2000.
- "Graduate education for the 21st century nurse." Poster presentation for the Fourth State of the Art of Nursing Conference, University of Nebraska Medical Center, April 4, 1999.
- "Psychological aspects of menopause." Grand Rounds, Department of Psychiatry, Broward General Medical Center, January 16, 1997.
- "Enhancing and expanding established partial hospitalization programs." American Association for Ambulatory Behavioral Healthcare Seminar; March 17–18, 1994; August 16–17, 1994; February 18–19, 1993; August 24–25, 1993; March 4–5, 1992, August 10–11, 1992.
- "Setting up partial hospital programs for accreditation and other key aspects of program success." Texas Association of Partial Hospitalization Annual Meeting, April 26, 1991.
- Kleinman, C., and Halperin, D. "Cults: Fact or fiction?" Southwestern Conference on Cult Issues, Dallas, Texas, April 10, 1990.

SELECTED
PUBLICATIONS

- Kleinman, C. (Manuscript under review). "Understanding men's advantages in nursing." *Nursing Leadership Forum.*
- Kleinman, C. (In press). "Nurse executives." *Journal of Health Administration Education.*
- Kleinman, C. (1982). State Board Review Examination: Grant-funded development of 240 test items for New York State nursing examination, City College of New York.

AFFILIATIONS

- Council on Graduate Education for Administration in Nursing, National Treasurer
- Institute for Nursing of New Jersey, Member, Board of Trustees
- Organization of Nurse Executives of New Jersey, Membership and Fund Raising Committees
- Bureau of Health Professions, Division of Nursing, Health and Human Services, Peer Reviewer
- New Jersey Student Nurses, Inc., Faculty Advisor
- East Orange School District, Member, Health Advisory Committee
- Healthcare Foundation of New Jersey, Clinical Fellowship Grant, Project Director
- American Organization of Nurse Executives
- American Nurses Association
- American Psychiatric Nurses Association
- Association of University Professors of Health Administration

Designing the Perfect Résumé

Even though content is important, many times well-qualified people aren't considered for positions because a poorly designed résumé didn't grab the reader's attention long enough to make sure the words were read. Just the opposite can be true as well. Even if your qualifications aren't the greatest, a well-designed résumé improves your chances of getting an interview because it stands out in a crowd of poorly designed ones.

The choice of overall style, font, graphics, and even paper color says something about your personality. In this chapter, you have already seen some résumé designs to help you find ways to express your unique personality on paper. Now, in the rest of this chapter, I will show you a few more.

If you want additional design ideas, then you should read *Designing the Perfect Résumé* (Barron's, 2000), with more than 260 sample layouts. It also covers in great detail the various elements of design.

Lisa Schenck

PROFILE
- Self-motivated sales professional with more than 15 years of proven experience.
- Top performer with a strong background in building new territories and using creative marketing approaches.
- Respected for the ability to get to the decision maker and close the sale.
- Demonstrated ability to create client loyalty beyond the sales relationship.
- Entrepreneurial thinker who works well independently or as part of a team.

EXPERIENCE

SALES REPRESENTATIVE, Waxie Sanitary Supply, Denver, Colorado (2000 – present)
- Sell paper products, chemicals, equipment, and cleaning supplies to large corporate clients, including The Pepsi Center, Coors Field, Invesco, Coors Brewery, casinos, hospital, and various other market segments.
- Formulated a two-year strategic sales plan for territory growth and built the territory from zero to $1.2 million.
- Created and conducted onsite training programs for end users focusing on the safe use of chemicals and equipment.
- Made sales presentations to upper-level management based on comprehensive needs analyses.

SALES REPRESENTATIVE, Unisource, Denver, Colorado (1992 – 2000)
- Sold paper products, chemicals, and cleaning supplies to large corporate and government clients, including hospitals, hotels, casinos, City of Denver, and Coors.
- Formulated a strategic plan for the territory and grew the account base by 350% through effective cold calling and account development.
- Created and conducted sales presentations to upper-level management, assessed their needs, and developed unique customer applications.
- Successfully regained former customers through effective marketing and follow-up.
- Designed and executed training programs for key clients.
- Achieved the President's Club through exceptional sales performance; ranked the number one salesperson in the Denver metropolitan territory.

SALES REPRESENTATIVE, Moore Business Forms, Denver, Colorado (1988 – 1990)
- Sold customized business forms to companies in the Denver territory.
- Increased sales to existing customers and developed the territory by 178%.
- Designed special forms to fit proprietary computer systems.
- Created a forms management program for the Poudre Valley Hospital.

SALES REPRESENTATIVE, Pitney Bowes, Denver, Colorado (1985 – 1988)
- Developed markets for Pitney Bowes copiers throughout 20 zip codes in the Denver metropolitan area.
- Consistently exceeded production quotas by as much as 250%, producing nearly half a million dollars a year in sales.
- Honored as one of the top five Pitney Bowes salespeople in the state of Colorado.
- Completed a comprehensive Pitney Bowes professional sales training program.

EDUCATION

BACHELOR OF ARTS IN BUSINESS MARKETING
Colorado State University, Fort Collins, Colorado

8641 Anywhere Lane • Newtown, Colorado 80124
Phone: (303) 555-1234 • Cellular: (303) 123-4567 • E-mail: lisor@protypeltd.com

SUZANNE DAVIS

210 Anywhere Drive ✦ Newtown, Colorado 80906
Home: (719) 555-1234 ✦ Cell: (719) 123-4567 ✦ E-mail: sdavis@protypeltd.com

PROFILE

✦ Experienced multimedia sales director with demonstrated success in:
  – Brand definition   – New product development   – Marketing plan creation
  – Market penetration   – Online advertising   – Strategic market research
  – Product positioning   – Franchise building   – Sales management
✦ Innovative thinker who is willing to step outside the box and take a risk.
✦ Proven sales leader with a strong background in building new territories and using creative marketing approaches to increase revenue.

EXPERIENCE

METRO NEWSPAPERS, FREEDOM COMMUNICATIONS, Colorado Springs, Colorado
Director, Major Accounts and Motion Pictures/Entertainment (May 2002 – present)
✦ Recruited by *The Orange County Register's* publisher to join the new Metro Newspaper Division, Freedom Media Enterprises (FME). FME is an integrated information and media company designed to service marketing and advertising needs in new and exciting ways offering one central account contact for three markets—*The Orange County Register* (Santa Ana), *The Gazette* (Colorado Springs), and *The Tribune* (Phoenix).
✦ Developed the business plan, sales plan, policies and procedures, execution, and implementation of the new organization.
✦ Developed and managed a revenue budget of more than $30 million.
✦ Grew incremental revenues to $3.1 million in the first five months of operation.

FREEDOM COMMUNICATIONS, Newspaper Division, Colorado Springs, Colorado
Vice President, Corporate Sales (June 2000 – April 2002)
✦ Recruited by *The Gazette's* parent company to develop a new business venture to generate advertising for 28 newspapers (1.1 million total circulation), 6 Internet portals, 12 Hispanic publications, and 10 military newspapers nationwide.
✦ Responsible for writing the business plan, policies and procedures, sales plan, and job descriptions.
✦ Hired, trained, and managed four account managers and an office manager.
✦ Created strategic and tactical marketing plans for the branding of Freedom Communications and generated more than $1.7 million in new revenue in the first year.
✦ Sourced contacts, developed sales presentations, made sales calls, and captured significant market share.

THE GAZETTE, Colorado Springs, Colorado
Director, Display Advertising (January 1996 – May 2000)
✦ Built a national advertising division from the ground up and managed major accounts, generating $24 million in annual advertising revenue.
✦ Hired, and managed a team of sales managers responsible for 40 account executives.
✦ Developed the *Home in Colorado* magazine that won the 1999 Addy Award for best in-house publication with more than four colors.
✦ Partnered with The Broadmoor (a Mobil five-star, five-diamond resort) to deliver *The Gazette* to guests every day; created a four-color, in-room *Broadmoor Magazine* for guests that generated significant income for the paper.
✦ Instrumental in securing advertising for the interactive division of the newspaper (colorado springs.com).
✦ Created partnerships with cruise lines and travel agencies to give the newspaper travel section a more national feel and to offer new opportunities to readers.

142

EXPERIENCE
(continued)

LOS ANGELES TIMES, Los Angeles, California
Advertising Sales Manager, Entertainment Category (May 1994 – December 1995)
+ Recruited from *The Orange County Register* because of the phenomenal success of its news entertainment section.
+ Managed a team of six sales associates responsible for selling advertising space in the entertainment *Calendar* section that generated $150 million in annual revenue.
+ Developed strategic plans for future growth and franchise protection.
+ Created and promoted unique online advertising programs that were ahead of their time.
+ Implemented performance management and team-building strategies that improved morale, reduced turnover, and increased individual sales revenue.

THE ORANGE COUNTY REGISTER, Santa Anna, California
Sales Manager, Major Accounts Division (June 1992 – May 1994)
+ Recruited, hired, and supervised a staff of 14 account executives.
+ Succeeded in growing revenue to more than $50 million a year from department, grocery, electronics, and small/medium specialty stores (Target, Macy's, Homestead House, etc.).

Retail Territorial Manager (June 1990 – May 1992)
+ Managed six regional sales managers responsible for generating local advertisements from retailers throughout Orange County.

Sales Manager, Entertainment Division (January 1988 – May 1994)
+ Developed and launched the Show Section, an entertainment tab that competed directly with the *Los Angeles Times Calendar* section.
+ Grew the insert from 80 to 124 pages through aggressive advertising sales.
+ Created significant advertising revenue with innovative partnerships, promotions, and special events.

Regional Sales Manager (January 1984 – December 1987)
+ Successfully managed local sales in the Huntington Beach, El Toro, and North County regions.

Account Executive, Display Advertising (January 1983 – December 1983)

Classified Account Executive (January 1982 – December 1982)

EDUCATION

SAN FRANCISCO STATE UNIVERSITY, San Francisco, California (1972 – 1976)
+ Completed three years of full-time undergraduate studies.

PROFESSIONAL DEVELOPMENT
+ **Landmark Forum Education** (2002)
+ **Community Leadership Forum**: Better Business Bureau (2001, 2002)
+ **Associated Press Institute**: Publishing Your Own Newspaper (1999)
+ **Center for Creative Leadership**: Leadership Development Program (1 week, 1998)
+ **University of Southern California**: Management Institute (1995)
+ **Aubrey Daniels**: Performance Management Training (1993)

AFFILIATIONS
+ NAA Advertising Committee Board
+ Better Business Bureau Board of Directors
+ CASA Fund Raising Committee
+ Denver Ad Federation

9980 Anywhere Trail
Newtown, Colorado 80809

Phone: (719) 555-1234
E-mail: kblack@protypeltd.com

PROFILE

- Experienced network administrator with broad knowledge of technical and training concepts, principles, and methods.
- Detail-oriented troubleshooter who gets to the root of the problem quickly.
- Known for the ability to create process efficiencies and getting the job done on time.
- Effective team player with proven communication and interpersonal skills.
- Hold an Interim Top Secret security clearance with access to Sensitive Compartmented Information (SCI).

TECHNICAL

Certification: Microsoft Certified Systems Engineer (MCSE)
Networks: Windows NT, Windows 2000, Windows for Workgroups, Exchange 5.5, Proxy Server 2.10, Microsoft System Management Server (SMS), Norton Ghost
Software: MS Word, Excel, PowerPoint, Outlook, Internet Explorer, Remedy, FrontPage, MS Mail, Netscape Navigator

EXPERIENCE

NETWORK ADMINISTRATOR (2001 – present)
Remtech Services, Inc., Cheyenne Mountain AB, Colorado

- Manage the daily operations of two classified networks with a total of 1,000 users, ensuring that resources are used efficiently.
- Maintain file servers, e-mail, backups, permissions, and security.
- Continuously monitor the network and troubleshoot any problems to minimize downtime.
- Create user accounts, write procedures, and handle network vulnerability issues.
- Install, configure, and optimize software applications and resolve conflicts using standard installation techniques and Ghost images.
- Develop packages to distribute upgrades and service patches using SMS.
- Discovered a physical problem on one of the e-mail servers, moved all users to the backup server, discovered another problem on the backup server, replaced them both, installed and configured the operating system and software, and migrated users to the new server.
- Recommended the purchase of a third-party administration tool (Hyena), which saved significant time.
- Currently helping to create an accreditation package for the network.

NETWORK ADMINISTRATOR (2000 – 2001)
Honeywell Technology Solutions, Inc., Schriever AFB, Colorado

- One of six administrators responsible for 3,000 users on an unclassified network.
- Installed, set up, and supported software products; installed service packs and hot fixes.
- Monitored network servers and responded to and resolved problems.
- Managed network/exchange accounts and share permissions.
- Provided input to generate and update project documents.
- Assist on special projects, such as network security, Windows 2000 testbed, and SMS packages.

LAN SYSTEMS ANALYST (1998 – 2000)
Honeywell Technology Solutions, Inc., Schriever AFB, Colorado

- Provided level-three help desk support for a 3,000-user, Windows NT/95 LAN via telephone, SMS, and on-site visits. Trained new users.
- Maintained a computer maintenance log documenting each user request, detailed problem description, and resolution. Analyzed information to determine potential for enterprise-wide problems/solutions.

EXPERIENCE

LAN Systems Analyst (continued)
- Assisted the network administrator with creating user accounts and share permissions.
- Served as the focal point for troubleshooting help desk DMS/Exchange and rewriting help desk procedures.
- Webmaster for the help desk intranet web page.
- Part of a team responsible for migrating all users from MS Mail to Exchange/Outlook.

STAFF ASSISTANT (1990 – 1998)
AlliedSignal Aerospace, Phoenix and Tempe, Arizona
- Rapidly promoted through four departments, culminating in Product Safety/Integrity and Materials Management.
- Provided first-line support for users experiencing PC hardware and software problems. Increased employee productivity by fixing 90% of problems immediately instead of waiting 24 hours for IS technicians.
- Surveyed department personnel to determine how applications would be used, then developed and taught customized Microsoft Excel, Word, and PowerPoint.
- Researched and recommended software solutions so employees could either telecommute or work additional hours at home, which improved employee morale. Installed 20 copies of pcANYWHERE and provided user training and help desk support.
- Designed and linked multiple Excel worksheets to provide monthly operating reports.
- Member of the team that implemented the total quality reward and recognition process in the Engines Department.
- Served as a member of the Policies and Procedures team that produced a desktop manual of the most important procedures for the credit administrators based on a survey of the department.
- Honored with seven recognition awards for commitment to teamwork, initiative, process improvements, and customer satisfaction.

EDUCATION

BACHELOR OF SCIENCE, INFORMATION SYSTEMS (1996)
University of Phoenix, Phoenix, Arizona

PROFESSIONAL DEVELOPMENT
U.S. Air Force: Windows 2000 Accelerated (November 2001), GCCS Advanced System Administrator (UNIX) (July 2001), GCCS Security Administrator (UNIX) (July 2001)
Solutech: Deploying Windows 2000 (January 2000)
ExecuTrain: Intermediate FrontPage 98 (July 1999)
New Horizons: Windows NT 4.0 Administration (October 1998)
AlliedSignal: Microsoft Master Trainer, TQL I and II Train the Trainer, Total Quality Facilitation, Situational Leadership, Managing Multiple Priorities, TimeMax Life Management, Managerial Techniques

Melissa Hardy

STRENGTHS
- Experienced loan processor and investigator with exceptional customer service skills.
- Responsible and dedicated worker who learns quickly.
- Effective team player with strong interpersonal/communication skills; highly proficient in Spanish.
- Proficient in WordPerfect, Windows 95, MS-DOS, MS Office, E-mail, and proprietary database and contact management software.

EXPERIENCE

DEALER SERVICE REPRESENTATIVE   1998 – Present
AmeriCredit Financial, Colorado Springs, Colorado
- Serve as a loan officer, working directly with car dealerships to sell loans to their customers.
- Call on 4 to 5 dealers per day in the Colorado Springs and Pueblo territory, generating sales of as much as $4 million per month.
- Supervise the branch during the absence of the manager.
- Promoted from customer service representative responsible for loan processing and verification of employment, credit history, and other loan data.

LOAN PROCESSOR/ADMINISTRATIVE ASSISTANT   1998
World Class Homes and Mortgage, Colorado Springs, Colorado
- Responsible for data entry of loan applications and Loan Handler computer files.
- Made weekly customer courtesy calls to update customers on the status of their loan.
- Answered phones and customer inquiries; set appointments with prospective customers.
- In charge of coordinating subordinations and preparing associated paperwork.
- Ordered titles, payoffs, mortgage ratings, appraisals, and evidence of insurance.
- Designed and updated database of all clients; organized paperwork in stacking order.
- Helped start the business from the ground up; ordered office furniture and supplies.

LOAN PROCESSOR AND INVESTIGATOR   1997 – 1998
Champion Financial Services, Colorado Springs, Colorado
- Processed vehicle loans, verified calculations on buyer orders, gathered stipulations from customers, and prepared paperwork.
- Verified employment and residency, checked credit ratings, requested proofs of income, and investigated incoming applications for completeness and accuracy.
- Communicated with dealerships regarding stipulations and rollbacks.
- Determined Blue Book and NADA values of vehicles.
- Made ten-day calls to remind customers of first payments and processed requests for deferred payments.
- Answered questions from customers, resolved complaints, and communicated with Spanish-speaking customers.
- Designed an improved filing system for home office loans.

SALES REPRESENTATIVE   1997
MCI Telecommunications Corporation, Colorado Springs, Colorado
- Sold long distance services and Continental Airlines frequent flyer programs.
- Set goals in a highly competitive environment.
- Received Player of the Month award for highest sales.
- Won a trip to Orlando, Florida and other incentives for sales achievements.

CUSTOMER SERVICE REPRESENTATIVE   1995 – 1996
Maxserve, Inc. (for Sears), Tucson, Arizona
- Provided customer service and telephone sales of appliance parts.
- Entered data into the computer and researched part numbers.
- Used communication skills to determine correct parts from customer descriptions.

ADDRESS   5390 Anywhere Drive, Newtown, Colorado 80918, (719) 534-0570

Carol R. Florio

P.O. Box 1234 • Monument, CO 80132 • (719) 555-1234 • florio@protypeltd.com

PROFILE
- Experienced landscape artist with a strong background in:
  - Xeriscape
  - Desert gardens
  - Water conservation
  - Low-water-use plants
  - Efficient irrigation systems
  - Wildlife habitats
- Proven ability to build trust and to sell new concepts to customers.
- Self-motivated professional with a strong work ethic and a passion for the environment.
- Effective team player with excellent communication and interpersonal skills.
- Knowledge of Windows, MS Word, Excel, Publisher, Outlook, and Internet Explorer.

EXPERIENCE

LANDSCAPING
- Certified Desert Landscaper, Phoenix Desert Landscape School, Desert Botanical Gardens.
- Experienced in the identification of low-water-use plants, appropriate maintenance of plants and irrigation systems, proper fertilization and weed control, and identifying and controlling plant diseases.
- Designed and installed a water-efficient landscape for a Habitat for Humanity property located in Gaudalupe, Arizona. Used xeriscape principles to design the landscape and installed an efficient irrigation system. Planted low-water-use trees, shrubs, and desert wildflowers.
- Renovated an old landscape to a new design compatible with the limited water supply of the Sonoran Desert.
- Recycled and relocated existing plants that were appropriate to the design and image of the new landscape.
- Removed high-water-use plants and installed new plants that functioned to provide shade, screening, privacy, seasonal interest, color contrast, and a wildlife habitat.
- Retrofitted the existing bubbler irrigation system to a drip system and upgraded it with an automatic timer to reduce water use.

SALES AND MANAGEMENT
- Successfully sold resale and new residential real estate. Licensed Real Estate Broker in Colorado.
- Consistently achieved annual Top Producer and won the Million-Dollar Producer awards.
- Built a client base through prospecting, referrals, cold calling, and direct mail campaigns.
- Demonstrated the features and benefits of properties and managed all of the details required to bring a transaction to successful close, including the negotiation of purchase offers and contracts.
- Responsible for long-range planning, profit and loss, budgeting, controlling costs, accounts payable, accounts receivable, operations, and customer service.

EDUCATION

CERTIFIED DESERT LANDSCAPER (1998 – 1999)
Phoenix Desert Landscaper School, Desert Botanical Gardens, Phoenix, Arizona
Successfully completed three semesters to earn the CDL designation.

UNDERGRADUATE STUDIES (1980 – 1985)
Arizona State University, Tempe, Arizona
Completed three years toward a Bachelor of Fine Arts degree.

JONES SCHOOL OF REAL ESTATE, Colorado Springs, Colorado (2001)

WORK HISTORY
Real Estate Broker Associate, Prudential Professional Realtors, Monument, Colorado (2001 – present)
Desert Landscaper, Phoenix, Arizona (1999 – 2001)
Real Estate Agent/Broker, West USA Realty, Phoenix, Arizona (1992 – 2001)
Real Estate Agent/Broker, ERA Realty, Scottsdale, Arizona (1987 – 1992)
Real Estate Agent/Broker, Coldwell-Banker Real Estate, Phoenix, Arizona (1985 – 1987)

Howard E. Hyde

1223 Anywhere Drive, Suite A • Newtown, CO 80906
Home: (719) 555-1234 • Cellular: (719) 123-4567
E-mail: hehyde@protypeltd.com

PROFILE

- Results-oriented senior executive with expertise in:
  - Organizational development
  - Strategic planning
  - Change management
  - Marketing/sales
  - Problem solving
  - Customer service
  - Line management
  - Staffing
  - Training and development
- Conceptual thinker who can see the whole picture, create a vision for the enterprise, and generate commitment from employees.
- Respected for the ability to lead business units through dramatic turnarounds and periods of high growth.
- Able to simplify complex subjects and communicate the concepts clearly to diverse audiences.

EXPERIENCE

PRESIDENT (1987 – present)
The Center for Customer Focus, Colorado Springs, Colorado
- Developed a successful business that provides consulting and training services to organizations desiring to become more customer focused.
- Created and presented workshops and seminars that helped client organizations dramatically improve their competitive advantage by creating more value for their customers.
- Analyzed client needs, developed innovative solutions, and served as a change agent.
- Developed measurement technologies that provided a systems approach to the measurement of a company's values and beliefs, its perceptions of service and quality, and the employees' perception of the organization's customer orientation.
- Successfully marketed services to clients such as Del Webb, NorthStar Print Group, Madison Fireplace and Lighting, Long Island Pipe, among others.
- Exceeded revenue and profit goals by setting high goals and mobilizing a strong work ethic.
- Recruited, hired, and supervised a staff of four employees in addition to independent contractors.
- Accountable for operations management, business planning, profit and loss, accounting, marketing, and customer service functions.

GENERAL MANAGER, MARKETING STRATEGY AND CORPORATE MARKETING (1985 – 1987)
Control Data Corporation, Minneapolis, Minnesota
- Selected to develop a complete plan for transforming the culture of the company from a product-driven organization to a customer-driven one.
- Conducted extensive secondary research at Harvard, Stanford, and the Kellogg graduate schools of business, and visited numerous customer-driven companies to broaden the knowledge base.
- Designed a measurement instrument to define discrete customer-driven factors and implemented a survey to measure the current culture of the company.
- Consulted with internal business units to strengthen executive marketing skills, develop marketing as a core competency, and improve financial performance.
- Created executive/employee development programs and modified human resource processes (compensation, performance appraisals, internal communications) to reinforce the desired culture.
- Developed and implemented a uniform strategic planning process that served as a model for other business units.

GENERAL MANAGER, MARKETING AND ACADEMIC EDUCATION (1983 – 1984)
Control Data Corporation, Minneapolis, Minnesota
- Managed the marketing department of a business unit that promoted computer-based education in the academic marketplace.
- Analyzed the market, defined market segments, and developed a marketing strategy to meet the needs of each segment.
- Instituted account planning processes and increased the sales force by 30%.
- Achieved 100% of goal and increased revenue by 152%.
- Created formal criteria for advertising agency selection, interviewed agencies, and selected finalists to compete for the account.
- Developed a new marketing communication strategy with the ad agency that significantly increased product awareness in the market.

**EXPERIENCE
(continued)**

GENERAL MANAGER, GOVERNMENT SERVICES DIVISION (1982 – 1983)
Control Data Corporation, Minneapolis, Minnesota
- Provided direction for a division that marketed educational computer services and hardware to the government sector.
- Developed and implemented the division's first marketing strategy and restructured prices.
- Reduced the number of market segments covered to focus on those segments with a higher growth rate and where the company could provide more value.
- Created a program to retrain unemployed steelworkers in Pittsburgh, which was so successful that President Reagan visited the operation to show how government and the private sector can partner to improve performance.
- Succeeded in lobbying to change federal legislation for the industry from cost-based to performance-based pricing.
- Produced the first profits in the division's history, increasing revenue by 166% in the first year and 183% in the following year.

GENERAL MANAGER, LEARNING CENTER DIVISION (1981 – 1982)
Control Data Corporation, Minneapolis, Minnesota
- Assumed full profit and loss responsibility for 52 education centers that delivered computer-based training programs to various market segments.
- Attained 130% of revenue objectives and improved the bottom line from a loss position to a 12% pretax profit.
- Promoted from General Manager of Field Sales Operations for the Business Center Division, which marketed computer hardware, software, and training programs to small business markets.
- Built the division from the ground up, including leasing and renovating the facility and hiring staff.

GENERAL MANAGER, WESTERN REGION (1978 – 1981)
Control Data Corporation, Irvine, California
- Managed four educational services divisions that included five Control Data Institutes, twelve computer-based learning centers, a consulting business, and a seminar business.
- Responsible for 175 full-time employees, as well as more than 100 supplemental employees and consultants.
- Took the region from the worst to the first region in the country by dramatically improving sales, profitability, and quality in all four divisions.
- Selected as the top regional manager; the region won 18 of the 23 top performance awards at the company's annual 100% Club event.

EDUCATION

MASTER OF BUSINESS ADMINISTRATION
Pepperdine University, Malibu, California
Graduated with a 4.0 GPA on a 4.0 scale

UNDERGRADUATE STUDIES IN ELECTRICAL ENGINEERING
University of Illinois, Chicago and Champaign-Urbana, Illinois

AFFILIATIONS
- Board of Directors, The Braas Company, Inc. (7 years)
- American Society of Training and Development, Current Member
- National Speakers Association, Current Member
- Colorado Speakers Association, Current Member
- American Marketing Association, Former Executive Member
- Sales and Marketing Executives International, Former Director
- Institute for the Study of Business Markets, Former Member
- The Pricing Institute, Former Advisory Board Member

PHILLIP W. SMITH

Home: (719) 555-1234 ▪ Cellular: (719) 123-4567 ▪ E-mail: psmith@thespringsmall.com
1234 Fossil Drive ▪ Anywhere, Idaho 80918

QUALIFICATIONS

- Results-oriented manager with a strong background in operations, marketing, sales, logistics, purchasing, and inventory control.
- Proven achiever with a strong work ethic and drive to succeed.
- Flexible team player who enjoys the challenge of change and is committed to lifelong learning.

EXPERIENCE

GENERAL MANAGER

JANIKING, Boise, Idaho (1997 – present)

- Purchased a franchise commercial cleaning business and grew revenue by 300% while holding down another full-time job.
- Generated contracts with 22 office and light industrial businesses through cold calling, Yellow Page advertising, word of mouth from satisfied customers, and JaniKing national accounts.
- Accountable for strategic planning, profit and loss, expense control, marketing, and customer service.
- Recruited, hired, trained, and supervised 12 part-time employees and one full-time assistant manager.
- Awarded Franchise of the Year for the Colorado region; selected for the President's Club (top 10% of sales nationwide); achieved Crown Club status (top 25% of sales nationwide).

PRODUCT & MARKETING MANAGER

COOK COMMUNICATIONS, Boise, Idaho (2001 – 2003)

- Managed the purchasing and reselling of inspirational products to retailers, mass merchants and nontraditional CBA channels.
- Developed annual and semi-annual marketing plans based on extensive market research.
- Wrote and managed a $370,000 marketing budget and provided input for the sales budget.
- Determined product assortment, purchased more than $3 million of inventory, and set prices to ensure profitability.
- Designed and produced displays, sales tools, and promotions to ensure constantly fresh merchandising of products.
- Managed a J.D. Edwards inventory control program that handled cost accounting, inventory reporting, sales forecasts, customer service, and tracking of sales and returns.
- Served as a liaison between Cook Communications and the third-party logistics partner.
- Provided direct customer service for independent distributors and handled their special order needs.
- Responsible for order fulfillment, shipping, and receiving.
- Managed an aggressive sales team that increased revenue from $4.5 million in 2001 to $6.2 million in 2002.
- Lowered cost of goods sold to 50% by negotiating deals with suppliers and ensuring lower printing costs for books printed on demand.
- Reduced inventory obsolescence to 1.5% of revenue by aggressively negotiating returns with vendors and reducing SKU counts from 1,150 to 470.
- Achieved an average of 75% sell-through for all products.

INVENTORY PLANNER	**COOK COMMUNICATIONS**, Eden Prairie, Minnesota (1992 – 2001) ■ Responsible for inventory control, purchasing, and database integrity. ■ Hired, trained, and supervised a warehouse manager and 12 employees. ■ Supervised moves of the entire operation from Eden Prairie to Denver in 1992 and then again to Colorado Springs in 1995.
WAREHOUSE MANAGER	**COOK COMMUNICATIONS**, Eden Prairie, Minnesota (1988 – 1992) ■ Managed the warehousing, receiving, and distribution of more than 1,150 items of inventory. ■ Worked closely with customers to ensure timely delivery of orders within a 48-hour shipping window. ■ Consistently shipped more products with fewer resources.
SHIPPER & ORDER PULLER	**COOK COMMUNICATIONS**, Eden Prairie, Minnesota (1986 – 1888) ■ Originally hired as an Order Puller but was quickly promoted to Shipper based on strong work ethic and attention to detail. ■ Responsible for order fulfillment, shipping, and receiving.

EDUCATION

UNIVERSITY OF DENVER, Colorado (1991)
Completed 1 semester of Purchasing Management courses

DR. MARTIN LUTHER COLLEGE, New Ulm, Minnesota (1982 – 1985)
Completed 2½ year of study toward a bachelor's degree in elementary education

PROFESSIONAL DEVELOPMENT
Inventory Control, APICS, 6 weeks (1996)

JULIE HARRIS, MS.Ed.

1234 Twin Gulch Court • Harrison, CO 80922
Phone: (719) 555-1234 • E-mail: julieh@protypeltd.com

PROFILE
- NASP Certified School Psychologist who sets high standards and motivates students to achieve success.
- Well-organized professional with extensive experience in special education populations.
- Effective team player with proven listening, interpersonal, and communication skills.
- Knowledge of Windows, MS Word, PowerPoint, Excel, and computerized IEP programs.

EDUCATION

Ed.S. IN SCHOOL PSYCHOLOGY (August 2003)
University of Northern Colorado, Greeley, Colorado
Relevant course work: Psychological Testing and Measurement, Abnormal Psychology, Theories of Personality, Seminar in School Psychology, Community Psychology and Social Systems, Legal and Ethical Issues, Psychological Consultation–Theory and Practice, Evaluation of Psychological Services, Child and Adolescent Psychology, Behavioral Approaches to Professional Psychology, Theories of Counseling, Intellectual and Cognitive Assessment, Family Systems, Infant and Toddler Neuropsychology, Evaluation and Correction of Individual Reading Problems, Computer Applications to Professional Psychology

MS.Ed. IN SPECIAL EDUCATION (1999)
Old Dominion University, Norfolk, Virginia
Emphasis on learning disabilities and emotional disabilities
Licensed Special Education Teacher K–12 (Colorado)

BACHELOR OF SCIENCE IN PSYCHOLOGY (1995)
University of Maryland, Heidelberg, Germany

CONTINUING EDUCATION
- Depression: Comprehensive Assessment and Treatment of Children, Adolescents, and Adults, Medical Educational Services, 8 hours (2003)
- ADHD: Beyond the Label–Assessment, Treatment, and Educational Interventions, Medical Educational Services, 8 hours (2003)
- Crisis Response and Intervention, National Emergency Response Team, 16 hours (2002)
- Threat and Suicide Assessment, CSSP, 8 hours (2002)
- Special Education Law, Law Advisory Council, 8 hours (1999)

INTERNSHIP

SCHOOL PSYCHOLOGY INTERNSHIP (2002 – 2003)
Harrison School District 2, Colorado Springs, Colorado
- Completed an intensive 1,200 hour internship in an elementary school, middle school, and alternative night high school program.
- Provided psycho-educational assessment, individual and play therapy, and direct/indirect consultation.

PRACTICUMS
- Cognitive Assessment, Gorman Middle School, Harrison District 2, Colorado Springs, Colorado (Fall Semester 2000)
- Personality Assessment, Colleagues and Families, Colorado Springs, Colorado (Spring Semester 2001)
- Individual Counseling, Buena Vista Elementary School, Colorado Springs District 11 (Fall Semester 2001)
- Systems Intervention, The New Horizons Alternative School, Harrison District 2, Colorado Springs, Colorado (Spring Semester 2002)

EXPERIENCE
SPECIAL EDUCATION COORDINATOR (1999 – present)
The New Horizons Alternative School, Colorado Springs, Colorado
- Coordinate special education services for 7–12th grade students with learning and emotional disabilities.
- Develop intervention, program, and transition plans.
- Write Individualized Education Plans (IEPs) and psycho-educational reports.
- Facilitate multi-disciplinary team meetings and taught annual classes in psycho-educational assessment at the District 2 New Staff Institute.
- Supervise, train, and evaluate special education student teachers as a cooperating teacher for the University of Colorado at Colorado Springs.
- Serve as acting administrator in the absence of the principal.
- Certified ACT administrator and Accommodations Coordinator (1999 – present).
- Member of the interviewing and hiring team for new teachers and paraprofessionals (1999 – present).
- Member of the District Literacy Team responsible for developing a new literacy program, including curriculum and tests (2001 – 2002).
- Member of the District Transition Team that provided career and continuing education services to special education students between 18 and 21 years of age (1999 – 2000).

HONORARIUM INSTRUCTOR (2001 – present)
University of Colorado, Colorado Springs, Colorado
- Teach Psycho-Educational Assessment to graduate students and professional educators in the Masters of Special Education Program.
- Developed and implemented a unique hands-on curriculum, examinations, and multimedia presentation materials.

SIED TEACHER (1998 – 1999)
Southeast Cooperative Educational Program, Norfolk, Virginia
- Taught emotionally disabled students in 7–8th grade programs for the most at-risk students (expelled, violent, economically disadvantaged, and prison populations).

MENTAL HEALTH WORKER, TEACHER'S ASSISTANT (1998)
Southeast Virginia Training Center, Chesapeake, Virginia
- Worked with nonverbal adults in classroom and residential settings.
- Taught sign language to improve the communication abilities of adult autistic residents.

DISCIPLINE COORDINATOR, TEACHER'S ASSISTANT (1997 – 1998)
Chesapeake Bay Academy, Chesapeake, Virginia
- Served as an intervention specialist for this private school for learning disabled and ADHD children. Investigated incidents, determined disciplinary actions, and developed classroom interventions to prevent future problems.
- Assisted in teaching second and third grade classes for the first half of the year before being promoted to discipline coordinator for the entire K–12 population.

SENIOR AIRMAN (1990 – 1997)
United States Air Force (honorably discharged)
- Desert Storm Veteran who served four years as a paralegal and three years as a vehicle mechanic.

AFFILIATIONS
- National Association of School Psychologists

153

Brandi Black

1234 North Corona Street
Colorado Springs, CO 80907

E-mail: thx1138@springs.net

Home: (719) 555-1234
Cellular: (719) 123-4567

SUMMARY
- Experienced buyer with a diverse knowledge of clothing, jewelry, accessories, and shoes.
- Proven ability to evaluate trends and to know what customers want to buy.
- Effective team player with strong communication and interpersonal skills.
- Knowledge of Windows, MS Word, Excel, Outlook, Adobe Photoshop, and Quicken.

EXPERIENCE

TERRA VERDE, Colorado Springs, Colorado (1992 – present)
Terra Verde is a lifestyle boutique selling upscale furniture, gifts, women's clothing, shoes, jewelry, and accessories in the historic district of downtown Colorado Springs.

Lead Buyer (1995 – present)
- Responsible for assortment selection and buying decisions regarding jewelry, accessories, and shoes. For two years, also served as the clothing buyer.
- Attend shows to find new lines and products, including among others:
  - New York: The Boutique Show, Accessoriestheshow*, Accessories Circuit, Femme, and Moda Manhattan
  - Los Angeles: California Market Center, New Mart Fashion Week, and LA Shoe Show
  - Las Vegas: The WSA Shoe Show
- Ensure excitement in each area by keeping up with trends and bringing in new and different lines/products.
- Reorder merchandise to maintain a constant flow of goods for sale, anticipating needs during strong sales periods.
- Receive and track merchandise, take physical inventory counts, and design displays.
- Process special orders and keep customers informed of status.
- Evaluate cost of goods sold and set prices to ensure profitability.
- Oversee the accurate pricing of inventory by staff.
- Provide sales support on the floor by assisting customers with their buying decisions.
- Open and close the store, handle cash and credit card transactions, and make recommendations for changes in processes and procedures.
- Facilitated a 400% growth in sales through assortment selection and accurate pricing.
- Helped the store to win *The Independent* newspaper's "Best of Issue" and silver award for "Best Jewelry Store."

Sales Staff, Back-Room Support (1992 – 1995)
- Greeted customers and introduced them to the store's merchandise.
- Used suggestive selling techniques to increase sales volume.
- Wrote sales tickets and accepted payments.
- Provided back-room support by receiving shipments, gift wrapping, and shipping orders.

EDUCATION

UNDERGRADUATE STUDIES (1993 – 1996)
University of Colorado, Colorado Springs, Colorado
Completed all but the senior year toward a Bachelor of Arts in Fine Arts

ENTREPRENEURIAL TRAINING COURSE (May – August 2001)
Small Business Administration, Colorado Springs, Colorado
Mi Casa, Business Resource Center for Women, Colorado Springs, Colorado
Course work included: Secrets to Becoming a Successful Small Business Owner; Legal Structure, Taxes, and Organizational Matters; Key Marketing Decisions and Research; Pricing, Financial Forecasting, and Credit; Marketing Mix; Marketing Plan and Analysis/Internet; Budgets and Projections; Record Keeping; Sales and Customer Service; Marketing Materials and Tools; and Business Plan Completion

ric Thomas

Phone: (719) 555-1234

4113 Anywhere Drive

Newtown, CO 80918

PROFILE
- Dedicated manager with a strong background in service and consumer product industries.
- Proven experience in business administration, event management, economics, and supervision.
- Energetic team player with the ability to communicate clearly and work well with others.
- Self-motivated professional with a demonstrated work ethic and dedication to lifelong learning.
- Experienced international traveler (four continents) with an appreciation for other cultures.
- Proficient in Windows, MS Word, Excel, Outlook, Access, Works, Netscape, and Telnet.

EDUCATION
BACHELOR OF ARTS, **University of Colorado**, Boulder, Colorado (1999)
- Major in Economics (Major GPA 3.6)
- Study abroad at Murdoch University, Perth, Australia (Spring/Fall Semesters 1998)

EXPERIENCE
BUSINESS ADMINISTRATOR, **Roche s.r.o.**, Prague, Czech Republic (2000 – 2003)
- Selected as a consultant for a contract to demonstrate Western business concepts for the Czech division of the third largest pharmaceutical company in the world.
- Conducted an internal audit of executive, mid-management, and staff-level personnel processes and made recommendations to executive management to improve the company's organic growth.
- Predicted a 7.2% growth in a shrinking market if recommendations were implemented.
- Evaluated stock supplies and recommended actions to save $27,000 in overstock.
- Designed the division's Web site to harmonize with corporate identity pieces.

EXHIBITION COORDINATOR, **Joly**, Prague, Czech Republic (1999 – 2000)
- Recruited by the AIESEC for a six-month internship with this exhibition company specializing in hunting and fishing events.
- Designed the layout and wrote the content for the company's web site.
- Planned and managed an event for 10,000 participants, including 40 international companies.

RESEARCH ASSISTANT, **Murdoch University**, Perth, Australia (1998 – 1999)
- Conducted research on the Phillips Curve, working side by side with the noted Dr. Robert Leeson.
- Analyzed data, created formulas, and drew conclusions relating to the Asian crisis and its effect on Australian higher education for the Center for Labour Market Research.

OWNER, GENERAL MANAGER, **College Pro Painting**, Denver, Colorado (1997 – 1998)
- Developed this franchise operation from the ground up, generating $80,000 in one summer.
- Recruited, hired, and supervised three crews with a total of 13 employees.
- Accountable for long-range planning, budgeting, controlling costs, collecting accounts receivable, and monitoring financial performance.
- Scheduled, planned, and coordinated large projects, maximizing resources and ensuring customer satisfaction.
- Developed new accounts through flyers, direct mail, referrals, and cold calling.
- Achieved the highest customer satisfaction rate in the four-state mountain region as measured by surveys.

PREVIOUS EXPERIENCE (1993 – 1995)
Foreman and Painter, College Pro Painting, Colorado Springs, Colorado
Line Cook, East Side Mario's, Colorado Springs, Colorado
Volunteer Youth Soccer Referee, Chargers Soccer Club, Colorado Springs, Colorado

Chapter 14

Electronic Résumés

Electronic résumés serve the same purpose as paper résumés but use a different medium—computers. They are a reflection of our changing times. It wasn't long ago that finding your dream job depended on who you knew, how good your résumé was, and how many newspapers you were willing to thumb through. Today, however, the rules are different.

The evolution of the Internet has created a nationwide job network that requires a new set of job-hunting skills. In 1995, only 5% of the 8,000 résumés Microsoft received monthly were sent electronically. In 1999, that number had changed to 50%, and the number of résumés had increased to 10,000 a month. According to Charlene Li of Forrester Research, online recruiting, including job-placement advertising, is expected to grow from $411 million in 1999 to $4 billion by 2005.

Because of this revolution, you need to add an electronic dimension to your résumé. There are actually three kinds of electronic résumés. The first is a paper résumé that becomes an electronic version when it is scanned into a computer. The second is a generic computer file that you create specifically to send through cyberspace without ever printing it onto paper—an ASCII text e-mailable version. And the third is a multimedia résumé that is given a home page at a fixed location on the Internet for anyone to visit at will. Let's look at each kind in turn.

The Scannable Résumé

With this first kind of electronic résumé, you innocently create a handsome paper résumé and mail it to a potential employer. Without your knowing it, that employer has implemented a computerized system for scanning résumés as they arrive in the human resource department. Instead of a human being reading your résumé and deciding how best to forward

> *The Internet has created a nationwide job network that requires a new set of job-hunting skills.*

it along or file it, a clerk sets your résumé on the glass of a scanner bed and the black dots of ink are turned into words in a computer. The paper is then either filed or thrown away.

Also falling into this class is your paper résumé when it is faxed to a potential employer. Instead of receiving a printout of your résumé, a potential employer allows your fax to sit in a computer's queue until such time as a clerk can verify and summarize the information into the same computerized database where the scanned paper résumés have been stored.

According to *U.S. News & World Report*, more than 1,000 unsolicited résumés arrive every week at most Fortune 500 companies, and before the days of applicant tracking systems and résumé scanning, 80 percent were thrown out after a quick review. It was simply impossible to keep track of that much paper. Instead of opening and reading thousands of résumés, companies can now scan them and sort them by keywords.

Recent sources indicate that most large companies are scanning résumés and using computerized applicant tracking systems to manage résumés received by e-mail and through the Internet. Even if they don't do it themselves, large companies turn to service bureaus to manage their résumé scanning or to recruiters to find potential employees for them, who in turn scan résumés into their proprietary databases. Even though this sounds like a lot companies, in actuality only 24% of companies nationwide scan résumés. According to a survey conducted by the Society of Human Resource Managers, 76% of all U.S. companies do not scan résumés.

As more and more companies establish a presence on the Internet and open up their computer databases to e-mailed résumés, the scannability of your résumé will become less of an issue. When you e-mail your résumé directly to a company, you have total control over whether or not your information is correct. You are not at the whim of a scanner's ability to read your font or formatting.

However, companies that scan résumés will continue to use their investment in this technology as long as they receive enough paper résumés to make the process worthwhile, so making your paper résumé scanner-friendly will continue to be important. That means choosing the right fonts and avoiding the common design errors that cause a résumé to scan poorly. Here are some of them:

Let's start at the top of your résumé and work our way down to examine the various elements that make a résumé scannable. What is the first thing you see on a résumé? The name, of course. The size and boldness of the type of your name should be larger than the largest font used in your text, but for a scannable résumé it should be no larger than 20-point type. You may use all capital letters, a combination of upper and lower case, or a combination of capitals with small capitals (LIKE THIS). Following is an example of a Times Roman Bold font in a few good point sizes for the name on a scannable résumé:

14 POINT NAME
18 POINT NAME

16 POINT NAME
20 POINT NAME

Avoid using decorative fonts like these for either your name or your text:

- **Broadway Engraved**
- *English Script*
- *Park Avenue*
- **COTTONWOOD**
- *Crazed*

- *Freestyle Script*
- **La Bamba**
- *Kaufmann*
- Linotext
- *Lucia*

Use popular fonts that are not overly decorative in order to ensure optimum scannability. Avoid fonts where one character touches another, since it makes it difficult for optical character recognition (OCR) software to determine where one letter ends and another begins.

Using reverse boxes to print white type on a black (or gray shaded) background is another mistake. Scanners can't read them and your name will be missing from your résumé! Here is a sample of a reverse boxed name:

PAT CRISCITO

Lastly, make certain your name is at the top of each page of your résumé. The clerks who scan résumés are often dealing with hundreds of pieces of paper a week—if not every day. It is very easy for the pages of your résumé to become separated from each other, especially since it is not a good idea to staple a scannable résumé.

Following are some samples of good fonts for a scannable résumé:

Serif Fonts (traditional fonts with little "feet" on the edges of the letters)

Bookman . . . . The quick brown fox jumps over a lazy dog
THE QUICK BROWN FOX JUMPS OVER A LAZY DOG

Clearface . . . . The quick brown fox jumps over a lazy dog
THE QUICK BROWN FOX JUMPS OVER A LAZY DOG

Garamond . . . . The quick brown fox jumps over a lazy dog

THE QUICK BROWN FOX JUMPS OVER A LAZY DOG

Minion Condensed . . . . The quick brown fox jumps over a lazy dog

THE QUICK BROWN FOX JUMPS OVER A LAZY DOG

New Century Schoolbook . . . . The quick brown fox jumps over a lazy dog

THE QUICK BROWN FOX JUMPS OVER A LAZY DOG

Palatino . . . . The quick brown fox jumps over a lazy dog

THE QUICK BROWN FOX JUMPS OVER A LAZY DOG

Times Roman . . . . The quick brown fox jumps over a lazy dog

THE QUICK BROWN FOX JUMPS OVER A LAZY DOG

Utopia . . . . The quick brown fox jumps over a lazy dog

THE QUICK BROWN FOX JUMPS OVER A LAZY DOG

Sans Serif Fonts (contemporary fonts with no decorative "feet")

Arial . . . . The quick brown fox jumps over a lazy dog

THE QUICK BROWN FOX JUMPS OVER A LAZY DOG

Arial Narrow . . . . The quick brown fox jumps over a lazy dog

THE QUICK BROWN FOX JUMPS OVER A LAZY DOG

Avant Garde . . . . The quick brown fox jumps over a lazy dog

THE QUICK BROWN FOX JUMPS OVER A LAZY DOG

Helvetica Condensed . . . . The quick brown fox jumps over a lazy dog

THE QUICK BROWN FOX JUMPS OVER A LAZY DOG

Myriad . . . . The quick brown fox jumps over a lazy dog

THE QUICK BROWN FOX JUMPS OVER A LAZY DOG

Optima . . . . The quick brown fox jumps over a lazy dog

THE QUICK BROWN FOX JUMPS OVER A LAZY DOG

It doesn't make any difference whether you choose a serif or a sans serif font, but the font size should be no smaller than 9 points and no larger than 12 points for the text. Having said that, you will notice that the fonts in the examples above are all slightly different in size even though they are exactly the same point size (11 point). Every font has its own designer and its own personality, which means that no two typefaces are exactly the same. Look at the difference between the 9 point Avant Garde and the 9 point Times Roman fonts below:

• Times Roman—9 point

• Avant Garde—9 point

You will notice that the Times Roman appears considerably smaller and is hard to read, while the Avant Garde is much more readable.

The key to choosing a font for a scannable résumé is that none of the letters touch one another at any time. This can be caused by poor font design, by adjusting the kerning (the spacing between letters) in your word processor, or by printing your résumé with a low-quality printer (i.e., old dot matrix printers). Even some inkjet printers can cause the ink to run together between letters with the wrong kind of paper.

Any time one letter touches another, a scanner will have a difficult time distinguishing the shapes of the letters and you will end up with misspellings on your résumé. A keyword search looks for words that are spelled correctly, so a misspelled word is as good as no word.

This is the same reason you don't want to use underlining on your résumé. Underlines touch the descenders on letters like g, j, p, q, and y and make it difficult for an OCR program to interpret their shapes. Take a look at these words and see if you can tell where a scanner would have trouble:

- The quick brown fox jumps over a lazy dog

- *The quick brown fox jumps over a lazy dog*

- The quick brown fox jumps over a lazy dog

- The quick brown fox jumps over a lazy dog

Related to fonts are bullets—special characters used at the beginning of indented short sentences to call attention to individual items on a résumé. These characters should be solid (•, ✦, ■) for a scannable résumé. Scanners interpret hollow bullets (○) as the letter "o." Avoid any unusually shaped bullets (□, ○, ✛) that a scanner might interpret as a letter.

While we are on the topic of special characters, foreign accents and letters that are not part of the English alphabet can also be misinterpreted by optical character recognition.

Even though you have probably heard that italics are a no-no on a scannable résumé, today's more sophisticated OCR software can usually read italics without difficulty (provided the letters don't touch one another!). The experts at Resumix state that their software has no problem reading italics, and my staff has confirmed that with tests. We have even scanned résumés typeset in all italics without a problem, although I don't recommend that simply from a readability standpoint. The key is to choose a font that is easy to read and not overly decorative.

Rely on white space to define sections. Scanners like white space. They use it to determine when one section has ended and the next has begun. Horizontal lines can also be used to define sections since they are usually ignored by more sophisticated scanning software, provided they do not touch any of the letters on the page. However, avoid the use of short, vertical lines since scanners try to interpret these as letters.

Don't use columns (like a newspaper) on your résumé. Scanners read from left to right and often have difficulty determining how to relate text to headings when the columns are the same width or when there are more than two columns. Although the keywords will be intact, your résumé may end up looking like garbage in the ASCII text version created during the OCR process. Using a narrow column of headings on the left followed by the text on the right doesn't seem to cause the same problem, however.

One nice thing about electronic résumés is that they don't have to be limited to one page. The more keywords and synonyms you are able to use, the better your chances of being selected in a keyword search. Therefore, it is better to have a two-page résumé with all of your skills and qualifications listed than to have a one-page résumé with information missing because you tried to conserve space. The general rule for an electronic résumé today is:

- New graduates—one page

- Most people—one or two pages

- Senior executives—two or three pages

One caution, however. The reader may decide to stop reading after the first page if something doesn't entice him or her to read on. Therefore, you should make certain that the meat of your résumé is on the first half of the first page.

Remember to keep your sentences powerful and interesting to read. Cyberspace doesn't negate the need for good writing. You still want a human being to read your résumé sooner or later!

Print your résumé on a high-quality, light-colored paper (white, off-white, or *very* light gray). Never use papers with a background (pictures, marble shades, or speckles). The scanner tries to interpret the patterns and dots as letters. This is a good rule to follow even for paper résumés that will never be scanned. Often companies will photocopy your résumé to hand to a hiring manager, and dark colors or patterns will simply turn into dark masses that make your résumé difficult to read. If a company has multiple locations, the original résumé may even get faxed from one site to another and the same thing happens.

Avoid using photocopies of your résumé. Original laser printed masters are best, although a high-quality inkjet printer is acceptable. Do not use a dot matrix printer since the letters sometimes touch each other or are not solid.

Print on only one side of the page and use standard-size, 8½-by-11-inch paper. The scanner cannot turn your page over, so the reverse side might be missed when the clerk puts your résumé into the automatic document feeder. That same process is the reason why you should not use 11-by-17-inch paper. The pages would have to be cut into 8½-by-11-inch sheets and the printing on the reverse side would not get scanned.

Don't fold your résumé since the creases make it harder to scan. It is much better to invest in flat, 9-by-12-inch envelopes and an extra two bits of postage to make a good first impression. Laser print and copier toner tend to crack off the page when creased, making the letters on the fold line less than solid, which a scanner could easily misinterpret. Staple holes can cause pages to stick together, so never put a staple in a résumé you know will be scanned.

The E-mailable Résumé

When you type words onto a computer screen in a word processing program, you are creating what is called a *file* or *document*. When you save that file, it is saved with special formatting codes like fonts, margins, tab settings, and so on, even if you didn't add these codes. Each word processing software (like Microsoft Word) saves its files in its own native format, making the file readable by anyone else with the same software version or with some other software that can convert that file to its own native format.

Only by choosing to save the document as a generic ASCII text file can your document be read by anyone, regardless of the word processing software he or she is using. This is the type of file you should create in order to send your résumé via e-mail.

An ASCII text file is simply words—no pictures, no fonts, no graphics—just plain words. If you print this text, it looks very boring, but all the words are there that describe your life history, just like in the handsome paper résumé you created to mail to a potential employer. This computer file can be sent to a potential employer in one of two ways.

First, you can send the file directly to a company's recruiters via an e-mail address. Second, you can use this file to post your résumé onto the Internet at a company's web site, to a job bank in answer to an online job posting (like at *www.monster.com),* or to a newsgroup. In any case, the file ends up in the same type of computerized database in which the scanned paper résumés have been stored.

There are many advantages to e-mailed résumés. First, they save you money over conventional mailing of a paper copy of your résumé with a cover letter. Second, they are faster, getting to a potential employer in only seconds instead of days. You also make a powerful first impression when you use today's technology to e-mail your résumé. And, lastly, your résumé will be accessible every time the hiring manager searches the résumé database using keywords. Your résumé will never again be relegated to languishing in a dusty filing cabinet.

A recent survey conducted by the Society of Human Resource Managers found that one-third of human resource professionals would prefer to receive résumés by e-mail, and your job is to make them happy!

The Multimedia Résumé

If you are a computer programmer, web site developer, graphic designer, artist, sculptor, actor, model, animator, cartoonist, or anyone who would benefit by the photographs, graphics, animation, sound, color, or movement inherent in a multimedia résumé, then this résumé is for you.

For most people, however, a multimedia résumé and home page on the Internet aren't really necessary. In today's harried world, most recruiters and hiring managers have so little time to read résumés that they are turning to scanned résumés and applicant tracking systems to lighten their load. They don't have the time to search for and then spend 15 minutes clicking their way through a multimedia presentation of someone's qualifications, either online at your web site or on a disk you might mail to them, so I wouldn't recommend spending much money having a home page developed or paying for server space to keep it online.

However . . . if it's free, it never hurts to add this networking tool to your job search. You can always direct your reader to your web site résumé by listing the Universal Resource Locator (URL—pronounced "earl") on your résumé and letterhead. That way, your reader has the option of going there for more information.

Most Internet service providers and online services provide some space on their computers for subscribers' own home pages at no extra charge. For instance, America Online allows its subscribers 12 megabytes of space per screen name to establish a personal home page in *AOL Hometown*. Your URL is your home page address and would look something like this:

http://hometown.aol.com/criscito

Granted, you don't have your own domain name *(http://www.patcriscito.com),* but it's FREE!

A word of caution about photographs and video, which are usually a part of the multimedia résumé. Human resource professionals try very hard not to discriminate, and a photograph that discloses your sex, race, or age makes it very difficult for them not to be biased. Hiring managers today would just as soon avoid even the hint of discrimination, so they may not view a multimedia résumé mailed to them on a disk for that very reason. Unless your appearance is a bona fide occupational qualification for a job (modeling, television, acting, etc.), then avoid using your photograph on any résumé, including your Web résumé.

The Paper Résumé Is NOT Dead!

The world of computers and the Internet will coexist with the more traditional world of paper and human networking contacts forever. Face it—computers generate more paper than they save! Therefore, you should think about having two résumés, one for human eyes and one for computer eyes.

There is so much to be said about electronic résumés. For more information about using the Internet to search for jobs and for complete instructions on how to create the three types of electronic résumés, check out *Résumés in Cyberspace* (Barron's, 2000).

Chapter 15

Cover
Letters

The first rule of cover letters: Never use a generic cover letter with only "To Whom It May Concern." With tons of work on your desk, would you be interested in such a mass mailing? You would probably consider it junk mail, right? You would be much more likely to read a letter that was directed to you personally, and so would human resources professionals.

The second rule: Every résumé sent by mail or fax needs a personalized cover letter even if the advertisement didn't request a cover letter.

The third rule: Résumés sent by e-mail don't need a long cover letter. Use only a quick paragraph with three to five sentences telling your reader where you heard about the position and why your qualifications are a perfect fit for the position's requirements. E-mail is intended to be short, sweet, and to the point. Then, cut and paste your ASCII text résumé into the e-mail message screen instead of just attaching your MS Word file (see Barron's *Résumés in Cyberspace* for detailed instructions on how to create and use an electronic résumé). Here is a sample cover letter for an e-mail message:

I found your posting for a Customer Service Manager (Job #12343) on the Internet at Monster.com and would appreciate your serious consideration of my qualifications. I have more than thirteen years of operations management experience that included budget analysis and tracking ($13 million), expense control, staffing, training, and customer service. I have succeeded in significantly controlling costs and maximizing productivity in all my jobs. My team spirit, ability to manage multiple priorities with time-sensitive deadlines, and strong communication skills would be true assets to your customer service program.

Pasted below is the text version of my résumé and attached is the MS Word document as your advertisement requested. I look forward to hearing from you soon.

Sincerely, John Doe

> *Never use a generic cover letter with only "To Whom It May Concern."*

167

This chapter will address several cover letter types. A letter to a recruiter requires different information than a letter in answer to an advertisement. A targeted cover letter that tells a story and captures your reader's attention is ideal when possible, but such letters aren't always practical (see the sample on page 180). Not everyone has the writing skills to produce an effective story, and the time involved in researching and writing the story would be impractical for mass mailings. A hard-hitting salesperson can write a dynamic cover letter, but not everyone is comfortable with that style and a good cover letter doesn't have to be "pushy."

Before we get into specific styles, let's cover some general rules that apply to most cover letters. The letters on pages 172–179 are general cover letters following these rules.

1. Customize each cover letter with an inside address (do not use "to whom it may concern").

2. Personalize the greeting (Dear Ms. Smith). Try to get the name of a person whenever possible. A blind advertisement makes that impossible, but in other cases a quick telephone call can often result in a name and sometimes a valuable telephone conversation. When you can't get a name, use Dear Recruiter, Dear Hiring Manager, Dear Search Committee, or Dear Sir/Madam.

3. Mention where you heard about the position so your reader knows where to direct your résumé and letter. The first paragraph of your cover letter is a great place to state (or restate) your objective. Since you know the specific job being offered, you can tailor your objective to suit the position.

4. Drop names in the first paragraph if you know someone in the company. Hiring managers take unsolicited résumés more seriously when they assume you were referred by one of their employees or customers.

5. The second paragraph (or two) is the perfect place to mention specific experience that is targeted to the job opening. This is your "I'm super great because" information. Here is where you summarize why you are absolutely perfect for the position. Really sell yourself. Pick and choose some of your experience and/or education that is specifically related to the company's requirements, or elaborate on qualifications that are not in your résumé but apply to this particular job. If you make mention of the company and its needs, it becomes immediately obvious that your cover letter is not generic. Entice the reader to find out more about you in your résumé. Don't make this section too long or you will quickly lose the reader's interest.

6. The closing should be concise. Let the reader know what you want (an application, an interview, an opportunity to call). If you are planning to call the person on a certain day, you could close by saying, "I will contact you next Tuesday to set up a mutually convenient time to meet." Don't call on Mondays or Fridays if you can help it. If you aren't comfortable making these cold calls, then close your letter with something like: "I look forward to hearing from you soon." And remember to say, "Thank you for your consideration" or something to that effect (but don't be obsequious, please!).

Story Letters

If you are planning a direct mail campaign to 50 or 100 or 400 companies, this type of letter is not for you. It just isn't practical. However, you will have to admit that the letters on pages 180 and 181 are great attention getters. For those dream jobs that require something special, this is the way to go. In a story cover letter, you must be able to tell a good story and write it well. If writing is not your forté, you can hire someone to write the letter, but you must still do the research and have a general outline of the story.

Letters to Recruiters

There are two types of recruiters: retained and contingency. The difference is that retained recruiters are hired by a company and are then paid by that company whether they ever find the right employee for the position or not. Contingency firms are also paid by the company but only when they find a good match and the job seeker is hired. Most recruiting firms don't charge the job seeker, which means they are working for their client companies and not *you*.

Because their mission is not to find the perfect job for you but to find the perfect employee for their client, they have little interest in communicating with you unless you are a prime candidate for a position they are seeking to fill *now*. Don't call recruiters; they will call you if they are interested. This affects both the beginning and ending of your cover letter. If you don't have a person's name, use **Dear Recruiter**. You should resign yourself to waiting for the recruiter to call you, so "I look forward to hearing from you soon" is an appropriate closing for a recruiter cover letter.

In addition to the "I'm super great because" paragraph(s), you need to add another paragraph just before the closing that tells the recruiter your ideal position title, industry, salary, and geographic preferences. Check the cover letters on pages 183–186 for examples.

Dynamic Letters

Job openings that require a certain amount of dynamic spirit—like sales—deserve a more dynamic letter. This can be accomplished in the opening paragraph. The rest of the letter is written like a standard cover letter but with a little more energy than usual. The last paragraph can be a bit more aggressive—you call the hiring manager instead of waiting for him/her to call you. See pages 187–190 for examples of cover letters that exude confidence and power.

Thank You Letters

According to a recent survey, less than 20% of applicants write a thank you note after an interview. Of the recruiters surveyed, 94% said that a thank you letter would increase the applicant's chances of getting the job, or at least help him/her stay in the running, provided the applicant is otherwise qualified. Fifteen minutes of your time and a first class postage stamp are very inexpensive investments in your career!

Thank you letters simply thank the interviewer for his or her time and reiterate some of the important things you learned about the company in the interview. Add some key qualifications that you forgot to mention in the interview, or emphasize some of the more important things you discussed. If the interviewer shared some information that gave you an insight into the company and its culture, mention how much you appreciated it.

A thank you letter should be short—three paragraphs at the most. Don't try for the hard sell. You had your chance in the interview. The thank you letter just reinforces what you have already said. See the examples on pages 191–195.

Letterheads

It is so easy to create a letterhead all your own and to make it match your résumé. Just copy into a new document the name and address you have already created for your résumé. It couldn't be simpler! It makes a very sharp impression when your cover letter and résumé match in every respect from paper color to font to letterhead.

Paper Colors

Color, like music, creates an atmosphere. Everyone knows that different colors evoke different feelings. Red can make a person feel warm, whereas blue does just the opposite.

Of course, you wouldn't want to use red in a résumé! . . . although an artist could get away with just about any color. As a general rule, résumé papers should be neutral or light in color. After 25 years in the résumé business, I have discovered that brilliant white linen paper is still the most popular, followed closely by a slightly off-white and then by shades of light gray.

Just make sure that the color of the paper you choose is representative of your personality and industry and that it doesn't detract from your message. For instance, a dark paper color makes your résumé hard to read.

In a scannable résumé, never use papers with a background (pictures, marble shades, or speckles), as a scanner tries to interpret the patterns and dots as letters, and the resulting information in the database can be spelled incorrectly.

The type of paper (bond, linen, laid, cover stock, or coated) isn't as important, although it also projects a certain image. Uncoated paper (bond, linen, laid) makes a classic statement. It feels rich and makes people think of corporate stationery and important documents. Coated stock recalls memories of magazines, brochures, and annual reports. Heavy cover stock and laid paper can't be successfully folded and don't hold the ink from a laser printer or copier very well, so they must be handled gently. All of these factors play a part in your paper choice.

Regardless of the paper you choose, mail your résumé flat instead of folded. It costs a few extra cents in postage and a little more for the 9-by-12-inch envelope, but the impression it makes is well worth the extra cost. It also helps with the scannability of your résumé. Thank you letters and other follow-up letters can be folded in standard No. 10 business envelopes.

John Q. Carter

1234 50th Street
Lubbock, Texas 79416
(806) 555-1234

June 10, 2003

Letter answering an advertisement.

Mr. John Q. Smith
Director of Human Resources
Continental Grain Company
123 Park Avenue
New York, New York 10172

Dear Mr. Smith:

I am very interested in the financial analyst position that you advertised in *The New York Times,* and would like the opportunity to discuss the possibility of working for your company.

I believe my experience in financial analysis, coupled with a strong quantitative and analytical background from my MBA and engineering degrees, makes me an excellent candidate. As you will notice in the enclosed résumé, I have spent more than three years working in various Latin American countries gaining experience with international markets and different cultures. I have also acquired an extensive knowledge of computer systems through my work experience and education.

I look forward to speaking with you soon. Please feel free to contact me if you have any questions or would like to discuss my qualifications further.

Sincerely,

John Q. Carter

Enclosure

MARCUS BAILEY

1234 Vondelpark Drive • Colorado Springs, Colorado 80907
Phone: (719) 555-1234 • E-mail: bailey@protypeltd.com

June 24, 2003

Letter answering an advertisement that requested salary requirements.

Human Resources
Boeing Corporation
1234 South Yosemite Street, Suite 470
Englewood, Colorado 80111

Dear Recruiter:

I am very interested in the position you advertised in *The Denver Post* for a Director of Worldwide Infrastructure Service Delivery Growth. My background and qualifications are an excellent match with your requirements.

My twelve years of experience in information systems engineering and management have focused on integration and organizational process improvement. During this period, I have developed outstanding leadership and management skills, compiled an excellent knowledge base of all phases of system and software engineering, and provided the vision for integrating future information technology into critical computer and telecommunication systems. Currently, I am responsible for infrastructure management valued at $10 million, including hardware, software, and networking systems with wireless and web technologies. The systems are geographically distributed, which poses service delivery challenges. My primary focus is now on reducing the resource conflicts associated with the performance, costs, and schedules of 15 projects throughout their life cycles.

Education in mathematics, as well as an MBA and a second graduate degree in operations research, combined with my extensive computer science experience, enables me to move easily between different industries that use information technology. This would be a tremendous benefit to your organization, providing more flexibility and proven technical leadership.

The travel required in this position would not be a problem. I am an experienced international traveler and would be willing to travel up to 40% of the time. My salary requirements are negotiable.

More details of my accomplishments are provided in the attached résumé. There you will see how my technical background and thorough understanding of information technology have been used to mitigate risks, improve competitive advantage and profitability, achieve corporate strategic objectives, and satisfy our quality service delivery goals. If your company could use these skills in this position, don't hesitate to call. I will look forward to hearing from you soon.

Sincerely,

Marcus Bailey

August 1, 2003

Ms. Marilyn Smith
Dallas Partnership
1234 Elm Street, Suite 12
Dallas, Texas 75270

> **Letter sent at the recommendation of a mutual friend asking for an informational interview.**

Dear Ms. Smith:

I am writing you at the recommendation of Mr. Bill Smith of the Arizona Economic Council in Phoenix. I developed a very amicable working relationship with Bill and the rest of the AEC staff during the short time I was there. As of September 1, however, I will be establishing permanent residency in the Dallas area and am seeking employment in the field of international marketing/management. Bill believed you would be a good person to talk with about the Dallas business scene and where the best employment opportunities in my field are to be found. Please note my qualifications:

- **Advanced Education – Master of International Management**: Graduated from "Thunderbird" graduate school, devoted exclusively to international business. Performed extensive graduate research and writing projects demonstrating my understanding of management, marketing, and finance on the international level.

- **Unique International Business Skills – Proficient in German**: Earned an undergraduate degree in German. Spent one year living in Freiburg, Germany, while studying German at Albert Ludwigs Universität.

- **Demonstrated Organizational Skills, Technical Competency**: I have a consistent record of achievements and honors. In academics, nonprofit organizations, and employment, I have always taken, or been asked to accept, additional responsibilities, thus reflecting my honest work ethic, skill in organizing work for expeditious completion, and ability to work under pressure.

Enclosed is my résumé for your review. Perhaps you may have a suggestion or two of whom to contact or where to look. Aside from my search for employment, I would genuinely enjoy meeting you, as Bill has spoken so highly of you. Since I plan to make Dallas my permanent home, I am interested in developing a relationship with the city and its people for reasons beyond employment. I will call your office next week to see if you may have 5 or 10 minutes to meet with me sometime in the near future.

Sincerely,

John R. Wright

Enclosure

JAMES A. CLEMENS, Ed.D.

1234 Country Club Drive • Colorado Springs, Colorado 80909 • Home: (719) 555-1234

March 26, 2003

Letter for a position in education.

Hazard, Young, Attea & Associates
1234 Waukegan Road
Glenview, Illinois 60025

Dear Recruiter:

Please accept this letter and résumé in application for the position of Superintendent of Sarasota County School District.

I recently completed my eighth year as Deputy Superintendent in Colorado Springs School District 11. My assignments and responsibilities have touched virtually every aspect of curriculum, instruction, finance, administration, personnel, training, planning, and development. I have now chosen to pursue a superintendent's position in a school district such as yours that can utilize this combination of experience, energy, enthusiasm, education, and expertise.

It is my belief that, more than anything else, public education is in need of leadership and not simply administration. I have demonstrated the ability to bring diverse groups together, motivating them to define strategically the community's views of the future of our school system. Under my leadership, School District 11—with 33,000 students and 3,500 employees—achieved increased student test scores within a short period of time and under severe financial constraints. My philosophy is simple and stems from this student-centered doctrine: ***All students can learn. All students want to learn. Success breeds success.***

Over recent years, the changes in public education have been sweeping, and there are more changes to come. As an education professional, I believe that I bring a unique set of skills, interests, and abilities to lead your school district into the future.

The enclosed résumé and letters of recommendation provide additional information on my credentials and accomplishments. I appreciate your consideration and look forward to meeting with you to discuss a mutually rewarding relationship.

Very truly yours,

James A. Clemens, Ed.D.

Enclosures

KITTY KOCHER

234 N. Grand Avenue • Pueblo, Colorado 81003 • (719) 555-1234 • E-mail: kkocher@protypeltd.com

July 21, 2003

Business and Technology Center
1234 N. Main Street
Pueblo, Colorado 81003

Dear Sir/Madam:

Leadership, strategic planning, market analysis, marketing, and business development skills are inherent traits that are fine-tuned through hands-on experience. For the past nine years, I have been using my business talents to help small business owners with marketing, labor issues, and legislative affairs. Now I am seeking a marketing position that will allow me to contribute to the community and its economic development.

As you will notice in the enclosed résumé, I have an extensive business development, marketing, and advertising background. I am currently the director of a destination marketing organization located in Manitou Springs. The advertising agency I operate provides media buying services, printing, creative services, and marketing research programs. The Internet service provider program I started has led to the development of a web site with more than 5 million visitors in 1999, and the traffic is growing. From 2000 to date, the site has had nearly 8 million visitors. Nearly $500,000 in sales was attributed to the web site in 1999. We tracked a $115 ROI for every dollar spent by our clients since 1996.

My diverse business experience has helped me develop strong skills in verbal presentations, meeting planning, financial management, community relations, data analysis, and special events. As with all successful small businesspeople, I can be "the chief cook and bottle washer."

I would welcome the opportunity to discuss how my skills would benefit your organization. You can reach me to schedule a personal interview by calling after 6:30 PM or by e-mail. I look forward to hearing from you in the near future. Thank you for your consideration.

Sincerely,

Kitty Kocher

Enclosure

Dynamic opening without the name of a specific person in the company.

176

Pamela Camp, CRCST

1234 Silver Drive • Colorado Springs, Colorado 80918 • (719) 555-1234

November 11, 2003

> Networking letter for an industry with limited openings.

Human Resources
Overland Park Regional Medical Center
1234 Quivira Road
Overland Park, Kansas 66215

Dear Recruiter:

I picked up a back issue of *The Kansas City Star* on my last visit to the city and noticed your advertisement for a Sterile Services Technician. Even though this position is probably filled by now, I hope you will consider me for similar future openings and have taken the liberty of including my résumé. My family and I will be moving back to the Kansas City area in January, but I could be available with as little as two weeks notice.

As you will see in my résumé, I have spent the last nine years as an Instrument Technician in a community hospital here in Colorado Springs. I have been totally responsible for the sterilization of surgical instruments and equipment for six operating rooms. In 1994, I completed the Purdue University Certified Registered Central Service Technician course and passed the national exams. Since then, I have kept my certification up to date with 12 CEUs per year.

The enclosed résumé will provide you with more information regarding my experience and accomplishments. I would welcome the opportunity to speak with you in person or over the phone to further discuss how my skills could meet your needs. I look forward to hearing from you soon.

Sincerely,

Pamela Camp

Enclosure

1234 East Platte
Colorado Springs, CO 80903

Telephone:
(719) 555-1234

July 12, 2003

> Networking letter requesting an internship or informational interview.

Stephen Smith
P.O Box 1234
LaJunta, Colorado 81050

Dear Mr. Smith:

John Smith, Professor at UCCS, recommended that I contact you. I have just graduated from the University of Colorado at Colorado Springs with an undergraduate degree in geography and environmental sciences.

My studies, combined with my Olympic training have been particularly intense. I often devoted more than 30 hours a week to my sport and still found the time to pursue my degree and earn a 3.4 GPA. Unfortunately, this rigorous schedule didn't afford me the benefit of an internship, but it did provide me with the desire to achieve and the belief that consistent training improves performance. Now that I have graduated, I would like to spend the next year working for a company like yours and learning all there is to know about the GIS industry. I am available full time in whatever capacity you need.

The opportunity to work for your company would be a real asset to my career, and I would appreciate your serious consideration of my qualifications. If you don't see a fit with your organization at the present time, I would still like to have the opportunity to meet with you or someone in your company who could take a few minutes to provide me with some ideas for how I might break into and succeed in this industry. Thank you for your consideration, and I look forward to hearing from you soon.

Sincerely,

Keisha Chamber

Enclosure

PATRICIA A. KUHARSKI

1234 San Juan Road, Apt. 12 • Sacramento, California 95833 • (916) 555-1234

facsimile
TRANSMITTAL

To: Kaiser Permanente

Fax: 1-916-555-1234

From: Patti Kuharski

Re: Security Services Manager Position

Date: January 12, 2003

Pages: 2

Message: I am very interested in the Security Services Manager position that you advertised in yesterday's <u>Sacramento Bee</u>. I am seeking new opportunities in a more dynamic environment that could use my skills in facilities and security management.

As you will notice in the enclosed résumé, I have more than fifteen years of experience managing security/safety programs with high-profile defense contractors. I am a recognized expert in program management and have a strong background in facilities management. My experience has also included supervision of personnel and I am skilled in team concepts and effective communication.

The enclosed résumé provides additional information on my work experience and accomplishments. I would appreciate the opportunity to meet with you to discuss the possibility of becoming part of this security services team. Thank you for your consideration. I look forward to hearing from you soon.

> Always follow up a fax with a mailed copy of the cover letter and résumé to ensure scannability.

JOSE CASTELLANOS

P.O. Box 1234 • Phoenix, Arizona 85123 • (602) 555-1234

June 26, 2003

A great example of a "story" letter.

Ms. Cindy Smith
College Relations Manager
Hallmark Cards, Inc.
P.O. Box 123456
Kansas City, Missouri 64141

Dear Ms. Smith:

It was in my hometown of Bogotá, Colombia, that as a teenager I came into contact with Hallmark for the first time. Even though I was not aware of the vision, effort, and commitment of resources that had gone into the Mother's Day card I had purchased, I was a happy customer. I never thought to wonder about the logistics of how that card had gotten to that small store or why a company more than 3,000 miles away was able to appeal to me, a kid from another country, culture, and language.

Hallmark's aggressive market penetration in more than 100 countries and its striving to provide employees with a supportive and challenging environment to best develop and apply their individual skills demonstrate to me that Hallmark is a company well worth entrusting with my career. In addition, I am impressed and attracted by Hallmark's commitment to supporting the communities in which it operates.

In light of Hallmark's international interest, you may be interested in my background. I started a small business in Colombia, which tested my energy, creativity, and initiative. The business quickly grew to be competitive as a result of innovative marketing and operation strategies. I have since learned to speak English, obtained a Bachelor of Business Administration from a U.S. university, and worked in several countries in varied positions, successfully adapting to both the people and management styles of these countries. Furthermore, in order to be better prepared for today's complex business environment, I am pursuing a Master of International Management degree, which I will complete in December.

It is my hope that my solid academic and cultural backgrounds, business experience, and interest in the international arena will convey to you that I have the qualifications to make a valuable contribution to Hallmark's efforts to remain the worldwide leader of the social expression industry.

I would like to be part of the Hallmark team that once helped me express myself through that card I gave my mother, and to take part in expanding the company to reach even more people all over the world. I would appreciate the opportunity to interview with you during your upcoming visit to Phoenix and hope that you will give the enclosed résumé favorable consideration. Thank you for your attention.

Sincerely,

Jose Castellanos

Enclosure

Gloria R. Clawson

1234 Queen Anne Way • Colorado Springs, Colorado 80917 • (719) 555-1234

July 21, 2003

A dream job with little relevant experience.

United Airlines (AFA)
Attn: F/A Employment
Box 66100
Chicago, Illinois 60666

Dear Sir/Madam:

I have dreamed of being a flight attendant since I was sixteen, but something has always prevented me from fulfilling that dream. Now that I've had previous experience with Western Pacific Airlines, I'm confident that I qualify for such a position. I would very much like to continue my career as a flight attendant, and work for United Airlines, which I feel is a well established and reputable organization.

With my twenty years of public relations experience, I would be an asset to United. I am a highly qualified individual who is ready to move forward into a more professional career. As you will see from the enclosed letters of recommendation, I am a very efficient and conscientious worker. I have a particularly strong desire to travel and work with people. With my outgoing personality and infectious smile, I know I would make a great addition to your team.

My résumé can only highlight my qualifications. A personal interview will assure you of my potential value to your company. I look forward to hearing from you so we may take the discussions of this challenging position one step further.

Sincerely,

Gloria R. Clawson

Enclosure

LORNA HURLEY

1234 Saturn Drive #123 • Colorado Springs, Colorado 80906 • (719) 555-1234

October 19, 2003

> Making connections with the feelings of the reader and explaining why the job would be a good fit even though the writer is over-qualified.

Human Resources
USAA
1234 Telstar Drive
Colorado Springs, CO 80920

Ref Code: PC-COS-1234

Dear Recruiter:

I have long been a satisfied customer of USAA, as was my father before me, so when I noticed your advertisement for Customer Account Professionals in a recent edition of The Gazette, I was immediately attracted to the possibility of working for USAA again. I was a supervisor in the Communications Center in your San Antonio headquarters for two years before returning to Colorado Springs for family reasons.

Although I don't know your current hiring needs, I hope to explore the possibility of working for USAA as a customer service supervisor. I was a supervisor at Allstate insurance in the customer and agency service department, and all of my positions have involved a high level of customer service for both internal and external clients. At Allstate, I reviewed detailed policy information and relayed that information to both the insureds and their agents. I am accustomed to working in a fast-paced team environment with conflicting deadlines and have good computer skills. My college degrees and continuing professional development have prepared me for success within your customer service department.

Even though you might consider my qualifications too strong for this position, I want to assure you that I would enjoy the opportunity to learn USAA's Colorado Springs business from the ground up. I would welcome the opportunity for an interview to further discuss how my unique skills could benefit USAA. Thank you for your consideration, and I look forward to hearing from you soon.

Sincerely,

Lorna Hurley

Enclosure

TONY POLACEK

1234 Bridle Trail
Pueblo, Colorado 81005

Phone: (719) 555-1234
polacek@protypeltd.com

November 17, 2003

Letter to a recruiter. Note the third paragraph that is unique in letters to headhunters.

Mr. Stefan Smith
President
Management Search, Inc.
1234 S. Cook St., Suite 12
Barrington, IL 60010

Dear Mr. Smith:

Is one of your clients looking for a Human Resources or Labor Relations Manager with a proven track record of success in both manufacturing and high-tech services industries? Then you will want to review my qualifications.

As a successful human resource generalist with extensive labor relations experience, I have become well known for my ability to improve employee morale and increase trust between unions and management. I have negotiated and administered several collective bargaining agreements and was often called in to diffuse stalled bargaining processes. My dynamic leadership style motivates change within the corporate culture and builds support from within the ranks. These skills, plus many more, would be true assets to any company whether they are unionized or not.

My target job is at the middle-management level with an innovative company that could challenge my skills in human resource management, employee relations, and compensation and benefit administration. I have no geographic preferences and would be open to relocation. My salary requirements would of course depend on the city, but I would anticipate a base salary in the area of $60,000.

Should one of your clients have a current or emerging need for a member of their human resource management team, I would appreciate your serious consideration of my qualifications as outlined in the enclosed résumé. I am free to meet with you at your convenience and look forward to hearing from you soon.

Sincerely,

Tony Polacek

Enclosure

LEE DAVID MILLER

1234 Amstel Drive • Colorado Springs, Colorado 80907 • (719) 555-1234 • E-mail: ldmiller@protypeltd.com

August 13, 2003

Letter to a recruiter.

Mr. Scott Smith
Office Manager
Korn/Ferry International
1234 S. Wacker Drive, Ste. 12
Sears Tower
Chicago, IL 60606

Dear Mr. Smith:

After a 25-year career in a number of senior management positions with high-tech computer/ communications companies in the Silicon Valley (and a short stint owning my own consulting company), I have seen many examples of great leadership and a few that were less than that. What seems to separate the truly successful senior executive from the mediocre is the degree of commitment he is able to instill in his people. I have been successful in building strong teams of productive professionals by creating comfortable, yet challenging environments that are stimulating and satisfying. Having participated in changes that have transformed the industry, I want to continue to be a part of this challenge in a senior leadership position that can take advantage of my in-depth knowledge of current technologies.

If one of your clients is looking for an experienced vice president or director who can motivate a team not only to meet but to exceed growth and financial goals, I am the person who can deliver those expectations and more. I am looking for a position that will continue to challenge me and give me the opportunity to lead a company into the 21st century. I have no geographic preferences and would expect compensation in the $130–175,000 range, exclusive of benefits.

The enclosed résumé will provide you with the details of my experience and accomplishments. I would welcome the opportunity for an interview to discuss how my skills and experience can meet your needs. Thank you for your consideration.

Sincerely,

Lee David Miller

Enclosure

184

HAROLD LITKE

123 East Oak Knoll, #12 • Lewisville, Texas 75067 • (972) 555-1234 • hlitke@protypeltd.com

January 11, 2003

Letter to a recruiter.

Ms. Sara Smith
Regional Vice President
Accountants On Call
1234 17th St., Suite 123
Denver, CO 80202

Dear Ms. Smith:

In today's tight job market, you undoubtedly receive hundreds of résumés every week from people seeking employment. However, you have a reputation for being able to recognize marketable talents, such as the ones I possess: diverse management expertise, a background in finance and collections, flexibility, commitment, and a highly effective management style.

I am a responsible leader with more than nine years of successful financial management experience. In my current position as the Investment Control Unit Manager for a multi-billion-dollar home equity services corporation, I manage $750 million in accounts receivable and nine employees. In addition to collections, I have experience in the banking, financial services, and home construction industries.

If one of your clients needs these skills and much more, please consider me as a candidate. I would like to live somewhere on the Front Range of Colorado. My minimum salary requirements are $60,000, exclusive of a bonus plan and company stock program.

Enclosed is a copy of my résumé, which provides more details regarding my experience and accomplishments. I am available to meet with you at your convenience to answer any questions you might have. I am in Colorado Springs until January 23rd, so please feel free to contact me locally at (719) 555-1234 or by e-mail at criscito@aol.com. I look forward to speaking with you soon.

Sincerely,

Harold Litke

Enclosure

DAVID F. KOVACH

August 16, 2003

Letter to a recruiter.

Mr. Thomas Smith
Executive Vice President
Anderson & Schwab, Inc.
1234 Seventeenth St., 2nd Floor
Denver, CO 80202

Dear Mr. Smith:

Are you searching for a goal-oriented sales manager with a reputation for building territories by as much as 40 percent per year? Then you've found him. I have been in sales management positions for the past 18 years and would like to continue my career in a regional sales management position somewhere in the Rocky Mountain states.

As you can see in my résumé, I have experience in the sale of chemicals, equipment, and instrumentation to the life science, research, and medical markets. My background in international biotechnology and medical research would be an asset to any company in the industry. I have consistently exceeded sales goals during all of my career and could bring this track record of success to a sales management position. My education includes an undergraduate degree in biological sciences and education, as well as continuing professional development that has included the Tom Hopkins Boot Camp, Systems on Consultative Selling, Mercury International Selling Seminar, and Anthony Robbins on Unlimited Power, among others.

My target job is at the regional sales management level in Colorado, New Mexico, Arizona, Texas, or Utah. My salary requirements would depend on the city, of course, but I would anticipate a base salary in the area of $80,000 plus benefits and bonus.

Should one of your clients have a current or emerging need for a member of their sales management team, I would appreciate your serious consideration of my qualifications as outlined in the enclosed résumé. I am free to meet with you at your convenience and look forward to hearing from you soon.

Sincerely,

David F. Kovach

Enclosure

JOHN M. DELL

1234 West Athens Street
Phoenix, Arizona 85123

Telephone: (602) 555-1234
E-mail: jmdell@protypeltd.com

May 11, 2003

Dynamic cover letter.

Human Resources Department
Conservation International
1234 50th Street, N.W.
Washington, D.C. 20036

Dear Recruiter:

I am a graduate student at Arizona State University. In the past week at school, at least five people have approached me to let me know that "the perfect job for me" was advertised in the Career Services Center. As I read over your job description for the Tagua Product Manager, I couldn't help but agree.

Your needs and my skills and experience are a perfect match. In fact, just two weeks ago I met with Coopena, a native Brazilian company operating within the Amazon rain forest to market locally made products in harmony with the environment. "Cause marketing" and international market development are my areas of interest.

My entrepreneurial experience and education are tailored to your needs. I have run my own business for the past four years. I create and market artwear with ethnic and environmental themes. My marketing is primarily through sales representatives and trade shows, which has resulted in sales to most major department stores (including Nordstrom, Marshall Field, and Macy's) as well as to more than 500 other accounts. In addition, my cross-cultural and interpersonal skills are conducive to effective teamwork within a multicultural environment.

My education at ASU has included emphasis on marketing and international market development. Often, my studies have centered on environmental issues. I authored an ethics paper on the Exxon *Valdez* oil spill. Currently, I am conducting an extensive market research project for a company selling food products for emergency aid relief to private voluntary organizations. My language skills include a proficiency in Spanish. In addition, this semester I have continued to work on market development for Tenneco to sell used equipment in Third World countries.

It is important to me to believe in what a company does. I plan to apply my skills and interests in assisting a company like Conservation International achieve its objectives. In addition, I can offer Conservation International the benefit of my creative and innovative thinking.

I look forward to the opportunity to discuss how my skills and education fit into your needs and objectives. Please feel free to call if you have any questions.

Regards,

John M. Dell

Enclosure

Michael C. DeWitt

Permanent Address: 1234 Edgepark Road ◆ Vienna, Virginia 22182 ◆ Message: (703) 555-1234
Present Address: Jan Luykenstraat 1234 ◆ 1071 CR Amsterdam ◆ The Netherlands
Home: (+31) 20-555-1234 ◆ Work: (+31) 20-555-1234 ◆ E-mail: dewitt@protypeltd.com

February 17, 2003

Dynamic cover letter.

Mr. Mike Smith
Vice President, Sales
BT North America
1234 East 52nd Street
New York, NY 10022

Dear Mr. Smith:

Would you have an interest in an individual who has generated over $50 million in global account revenues for a telecommunications leader, and who recently played a key role in the success of a new BT European joint venture? If so, I'd like to speak with you about how I can employ these skills and my knowledge of MCI/WorldCom to help BT North America achieve its revenue and business objectives in the new global marketplace.

As a successful sales and business development manager with MCI, I have a proven track record of delivering significant revenue and profit growth by building value propositions for advanced voice, data, and Internet applications. These skills have placed me within the top one percent of MCI's global sales force on three separate occasions.

In my current assignment as a member of the senior management team for Telfort in the Netherlands, I direct a group that, in just six months time, has been instrumental in contributing over $10 million in revenue to this successful startup.

With my overseas assignment drawing to a close in April 2003, I have a strong interest in pursuing opportunities within BT North America. Should you have a current or emerging need for a proven contributor to your management team, I would appreciate your serious consideration of my qualifications outlined in the enclosed résumé.

My present travel plans call for me to be in the United States from 2/20 through 3/2. I would welcome the opportunity to meet with you in person and will contact you shortly to determine if this is convenient for you. I look forward to hearing from you soon.

Sincerely,

Michael C. DeWitt

Enclosure

DETLEF E. SAPETA

1234 Gilcrest Road ◆ Colorado Springs, CO 80906 ◆ (719) 555-1234 ◆ E-mail: sapeta@protypeltd.com

March 4, 2003

Ms. Cherlynn M. Smith
Staff Recruiter
A la Carte International, West
1234 E. Girard Drive
Aurora, CO 80013

Dear Ms. Smith:

Are you in need of a catalyst for change . . . someone who can turn around unprofitable operations and generate guest and employee loyalty? Then you have found him! I am ready to bring my considerable experience in hotel management to A la Carte International and would appreciate your serious consideration of my qualifications:

- High-level hotel management experience, broad operational knowledge, flexibility, commitment, and a dynamic, innovative leadership style.
- More than 20 years of successful experience at both the General Manager and District Manager levels.
- Background in multi-property management—I was the Managing Director of four hotels with more than 700 rooms, including one 4-star, 4-diamond property.
- Experience in managing budgets of up to $50 million and operations generating 32–37% in gross profits annually.
- Very persuasive speaker and business negotiator who routinely makes presentations at the highest levels of management.

If A la Carte could use these skills and much more, please consider me as a candidate. I have spent the last two years managing a family business and doing some hotel consulting work, but I have hotel management in my blood and I want to get back to work **now**! I have no real geographic preferences and am very flexible. I have lived and traveled all over the world and find that every location has its own unique charm.

Enclosed is a copy of my résumé that provides more details regarding my experience and accomplishments. I am available to meet with you at your convenience to answer any questions you might have and look forward to speaking with you soon.

Sincerely,

Detlef E. Sapeta

Enclosure

Deborah F. Buehler

1234 Lexington Park Drive • Colorado Springs, CO 80920
Phone: (719) 555-1234 • E-mail: dfbuehler@protypeltd.com

May 15, 2003

Dynamic cover letter.

KVUU 99.9 Radio
Citadel Radio Center
Tiffany Square
1234 Corporate Drive, Suite 123
Colorado Springs, CO 80919

Dear Recruiter:

I heard on one of your radio shows today that you are searching for a goal-oriented Account Executive. You've found her.

After fourteen years in the sale of educational services, I have a proven track record of exceeding sales goals and generating profits for my employer. I am especially adept at making sales presentations and enjoy the one-on-one interaction of working directly with the customer. Besides my sales experience, I have a strong background in management and administration. That experience helps me to organize territories and supervise other sales representatives.

The enclosed résumé will give you more information on my experience and accomplishments. I would welcome the opportunity for an interview to further explore how my skills and experience could benefit KVUU. I look forward to hearing from you soon.

Sincerely,

Deborah F. Buehler

Enclosure

Liz Steele

1234 Ashwood Circle
Colorado Springs, CO 80906
Phone: (719) 555-1234
E-mail: lsteele@protypeltd.com

June 7, 2003

Thank you letter that
drops the name of the
recipient's manager.

Ms. Jeanine Smith
Director of Sales and Marketing
The Cliff House
1234 Canon Avenue
Manitou Springs, Colorado 80829

Dear Ms. Smith:

Thank you for taking the time to interview me for the Sales Manager position at The Cliff
House. As we discussed, I have built two successful businesses from the ground up and am
very comfortable making cold calls, networking, and building a clientele from scratch. One
of those businesses was a travel agency, where I worked closely with my counterparts in the
hospitality industry and made high-level presentations to corporate prospects. This
experience would translate well into the hotel industry here in the Colorado Springs area.

I had the unexpected pleasure of speaking with Craig Hartman on Friday, May 28, and got
a positive feeling for the management culture at The Cliff House even before meeting you. I
know that I would be a good fit in the Sales Manager position. Enclosed is a copy of my
reference list, as you requested. If you have any further questions, feel free to give me a call.
I look forward to hearing from you soon.

Sincerely,

Liz Steele

Enclosure

Regina M. Contrell

1234 Blodgett Drive
Colorado Springs, CO 80919

E-mail: contrell@protypeltd.com

Phone (719) 555-1234
Fax (719) 555-1234

February 1, 2003

> Thank you letter for an interview
> and expression of continued interest.

Ms. Joan C. Smith
Assistant Superintendent
Elementary School Education
Virginia Beach City Public Schools
1234 George Mason Drive
Virginia Beach, Virginia 23456-0038

Dear Ms. Smith:

Thank you so much for considering my application for the Principal position at New Castle Elementary School. I was excited about our interview and the quality of your district, and I understand completely your choice of an existing principal within your district for this position. I wanted to let you know that I am still very much interested in a position in the Virginia Beach City Public Schools and would appreciate your consideration of my qualifications for the other Principal positions you are advertising on your web site.

As we discussed in my interview, I lived for twenty years in the Virginia Beach area and served as an administrator in the Norfolk Public Schools for thirteen years. My husband's business interests are bringing us back to Virginia soon, and I can be available with little notice. I appreciate your consideration of my qualifications and look forward to hearing from you soon.

Sincerely,

Regina M. Contrell

Enclosure

MICHAEL A. STEVENS

1234 Plainview Place • Manitou Springs, Colorado 80829 • (719) 555-1234

November 3, 2003

Mr. Tom Smith
Volt Services Group
1234 South Tejon, Suite 12
Colorado Springs, Colorado 80903

Dear Tom:

I wanted to thank you for the opportunity to meet with you last Thursday to discuss sales opportunities with your company. I hope our meeting went well enough for us to move forward in the process. I know you have interviewed many qualified candidates, but I wanted to let you know that I am the best candidate for the position. After more than ten years in sales, I would bring to Volt a proven record of success that helped me to achieve the top 10 percent of sales representatives for both MCI and California Casualty Insurance.

Thank you again for your time and consideration. I look forward to hearing from you soon.

Sincerely,

Michael A. Stevens

BEN VISCON
1234 42nd Avenue, S.W., Seattle, Washington 98136
Telephone: (206) 555-1234

November 16, 2003

Ms. Janet Smith
REI
P.O. Box 1234
Sumner, Washington 98390

Dear Janet:

It was a pleasure meeting you today, and I appreciate your taking the time to discuss career opportunities at rei.com with me. The growth of your company in the past few years is very exciting and I would very much like to become part of that success.

As we discussed, I would welcome the opportunity to take my eleven years of retail buying, planning, and management to the next level with e-commerce. I have a proven background in operations management, planning, and product management and could bring that experience to rei.com.

Thank you again for your consideration, and I look forward to hearing from you soon.

Sincerely,

Ben Viscon

Anne K. Mori

1234 Camfield Circle ◆ Colorado Springs, Colorado 80920 ◆ (719) 555-1234

January 17, 2003

Ms. Dana Smith
Administrator
Laurel Manor Care Center
1234 S. Chelton Road
Colorado Springs, Colorado 80910

Dear Dana:

I very much enjoyed having the opportunity to meet you and to tour Laurel Manor recently. I would like to thank you for taking the time to show me around and answer a few questions. Your facility impressed me as a warm, caring place for families to bring their loved ones and a pleasant working environment for employees.

I am very interested in interviewing for the Rehab Manager position you have advertised. I have had more than 12 years of experience as a speech-language pathologist and have spent the past year working in long-term care. I have worked very closely with our rehab director and have a working knowledge of OBRA, Medicare guidelines, and documentation, as well as managed care contracts, which greatly affect how and what we do in therapy!

Enclosed is a copy of my résumé, which should give you a broader picture of my clinical and supervisory experience. I look forward to hearing from you.

Sincerely,

Anne K. Mori

Enclosure

Index